A FATHER AND SON'S YUKON BUSH PILOT ADVENTURES

Also by Larry Whitesitt

Flight of the Red Beaver

Northern Flight of Dreams

Higher Than Eagles
Spokane's World War II Pilots

Northern Flight of Dreams
DVD of last 11 chapters

Books and DVD available at Amazon.com

A FATHER AND SON'S
YUKON BUSH PILOT ADVENTURES

LARRY WHITESITT

Whitesitt Aviation Books • Fairfield, Washington

Published by
Whitesitt Aviation Books
PO Box 49
Fairfield, Washington 99012

A Father and Son's Yukon Bush Pilot Adventures
Copyright 2019 Larry Whitesitt
All rights reserved

Manuscript preparation by: Lynn Schafer

ISBN: 978-0-9629085-6-9

Printed in the United States of America

First Edition

Front cover: Scott and Larry standing by the Red Beaver at the South Nahanni River, Northwest Territories

Back cover: The Red Beaver flying north of Watson Lake, Yukon.

Interior has 100 photos chronicling Larry & Scott's time in the Yukon.

Dedicated to Scott, Stacy,
Daniel, Kaitlyn and Gavin

Contents

The Yukon is a beautiful, rugged land, mostly wilderness that extends north from Mt. Logan, Canada's highest mountain to the Arctic Sea.

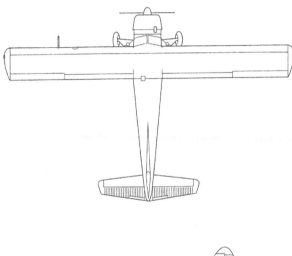

Beaver specifications

Beaver Mk. I
1,631 built

LANDPLANE

ENGINE
One 450-hp Pratt & Whitney
R-985 AN-6B or AN-14B Wasp Jr.

DIMENSIONS
Wing span: 48 ft (14.6 m)
Length: 30 ft 4 in (9.2 m)
Wing area: 250 sq ft (23.2 sq m)

OVERALL HEIGHT
Wheels: 9 ft (2.7 m)
Skis: 9 ft 6 in (2.9 m)

WEIGHTS
Landplane
Basic weight: 3,000 lb (1,360 kg)
Disposable load: 2,100 lb (953 kg)
Gross weight: 5,100 lb (2,313 kg)
Ski-wheels
Basic weight: 3,223 lb (1,465 kg)
Disposable load: 1,867 lb (847 kg)
Gross weight: 5,100 lb (2,313 kg)

PERFORMANCE
Maximum speed: 160 mph (257 km/hr)
Cruise: 130 mph (209 km/hr) at
    5,000 ft (1,524 m)
Initial rate of climb: 1,020 ft/min (311 m/min)
Service ceiling: 18,000 ft (5,486 m)

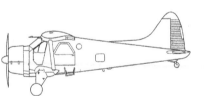

PROLOGUE

Early in July, 1972, I prepared to fly on a rescue mission with my cheerful son Scott as co-pilot in my favorite red Beaver float plane CF-IBP. We received an emergency call from one of Chuck Hayward's hunting guides on an island in the South Nahanni River, Northwest Territories. He said another guide was swimming his horse across the river but the horse drowned, and the guide couldn't swim but made it to a sandbar. The river was in flood stage and rising. Another pilot, John Poizer, flew a Super Cub on floats and rescued the guide.

I was told to fly to Chuck Hayward's hunting camp on Little Dal Lake and fly Chuck to the island. We picked up Chuck and landed on the Nahanni River. The horses refused to swim in the river after watching the horse drown. We built a fence out of brush into the river, hoping to get them to swim. We shouted, shot guns and the guides on horseback chased the horses into the river, but the horses just walked around the barrier and ran to the end of the island.

I flew Chuck to a lake where he had a boat and outboard motor. We tied the boat to the top of the float and flew back to the island. Chuck tied a rope to a horse and connected it to the boat, and with a guide started pulling the horse across the river. After pulling a few horses across, the boat capsized and was lost. Chuck and the guide managed to swim to the north bank of the river and grab a tree that had fallen into the river and climbed up to the beach. I taxied the Beaver across the river and picked up Chuck and the guide, who were soaking wet but unharmed. The other horses finally swam across the river.

Scott and I spent two days on the rescue mission and slept in the Beaver at night before returning to Watson Lake.

From the age of 10 to 15 years old, (1970-1975), when school let out, Scott spent the summer flying with me in float planes out of Watson Lake, Yukon. I'm a Flight Instructor, and once airborne when we had no passengers, I let him fly. Scott was a cautious, safe pilot and took flying seriously.

Scott soloed in a glider at age 14 and on his 16th birthday soloed in a Piper J-3 Cub at Henley Aerodrome, Athol, Idaho.

Some of the stories in this book were in my first two books, *Flight of the Red Beaver* published in 1990 and *Northern Flight of Dreams* published in 2004 by Whitesitt Aviation Books.

Chapter 1

"Yukon Dream"

The Yukon is a beautiful, rugged land, mostly wilderness that extends north from Mt. Logan, Canada's highest mountain to the Arctic Sea.

The Call of the Wild, written by Jack London, was my favorite book as a young boy shortly after World War II. The story was about a large sled dog named Buck and took place in the Yukon. Buck's owner was killed by Indians, and he escaped into the wilderness and became the leader of a wolf pack.

Jack London was a gold seeker during that great Klondike Gold Rush of 1896-1899 in the Yukon. He was one of thousands of Klondikers who hiked over the Chilkoot Pass out of Skagway, Alaska, built a boat and drifted down the Yukon River to Dawson City, which at that time was the capital of the Yukon.

He built a log cabin on Henderson Creek and dug for gold. Jack didn't find gold, but his experience as a Klondiker gave him the material to write the books about the Yukon, which was his 'pot of gold.' His log cabin on Henderson Creek has been moved to Dawson City next to Robert Service's cabin. Service was the great poet of the Klondike Gold Rush.

On the radio I listened to Sergeant Preston of the Yukon, who was a Mountie in the North West Mounted Police out of Dawson City during the Klondike Gold Rush. Sergeant Preston's lead sled dog was Yukon King. The good Sergeant's voice could be heard above a snowstorm yelling, "Mush, you huskies, mush; onward King, onward," as they chased a lawbreaker across the frozen north. You could send the top of a cereal box and money to the radio station and receive a deed for one square inch of land in the Yukon. My boyhood dream was to go to the land called "The Yukon."

The Yukon is a vast, rugged land that extends north over 600 miles from the British Columbia border to the Arctic Ocean called the Beaufort Sea, from Alaska on its western border east to the Northwest Territories, on its southern border is 583 miles, and the northern border along the Arctic Sea is very narrow. The Yukon has 186,000 square miles. Its population was about 23,500, one person for every eight square miles in the 1970s.

Yukon is an Indian name meaning "The Great River" It is the coldest area in North America, and minus 60 degrees is common. In the southwest corner of the Yukon is a pristine wilderness called Kluane National Park, so remote that 90 percent of its features are unnamed. The park is over 8,000 square miles, half the size of Switzerland. Mt. Logan is the highest mountain in the park, and in Canada with an elevation of 19,551 feet, and ten other peaks are over 15,000. There are more than 2,000 glaciers, and it is the largest ice field on the planet outside the polar region. More than 700 kinds of flora grow here.

The Yukon has a large population of big game animals, including the white Dall sheep, wolves, moose, deer, grizzly bears, caribou and, along the Arctic coast, polar bears. The Porcupine Caribou herd of about 180,000 migrate by the Indian village of Old Crow in the Yukon along the Porcupine River in the spring on their journey northwest to Alaska, where they calve and then return to the Yukon and Northwest Territories in the fall.

The Old Crow Indians depend on the caribou for food, as well as moose and salmon. The Indian long riverboats with outboard motors are pulled up on the beach of the Porcupine River in front of the village. The river is their highway during the summer with their boats. In the winter they use snowmobiles, and before that they used dog sleds. They still use dog sleds for racing in the winter. They race their dog sleds at White-horse, the capital of the Yukon during the long cold winter months.

The adjoining Northwest Territories bordering on the east side of the Yukon had a population of about 52,200, one person for every 25 square miles. The Yukon and Northwest Territories, both Canadian Territories, covered 1,508,900 square miles, three times larger than Alaska, the size of the lower 48 United States in the 1970s. Since then a large portion of the Northwest Territories east of Yellowknife, the capital, has been renamed Nunavut, home of the native Inuits. In Alaska the Inuits are sometimes called Eskimos.

During World War II, I became fascinated with airplanes and flying while watching DC-3s and fighters fly across the sky. When a plane flew over, I looked up in boyhood wonder, and I still do so as a much older boy. The first toy I remember playing with was a metal single-engine military plane, which I can still see in my mind's eye. In 1944 in Sandpoint, Idaho where I started the first grade, I built my first flying model called a German Stuka Dive Bomber. It was constructed of a balsa wood frame covered with tissue paper and several coats of airplane dope, and it had a wooden prop connected to two rubber bands. I launched it off our front porch, and it crashed. My father drove a bus with sailors from Sandpoint to Farragut Naval Training Center (boot camp) located by Pend Oreille Lake. My grandfather, William C. Rydblom, had a 35-foot yacht at the lake named Susan Joe after two of his daughters. The Navy bought his yacht.

On Saturday us kids would walk to the Panida Theater downtown to see a movie for ten cents. We moved back to Spokane a few months after school started, and I went to the first grade at Stevens Grade School. My younger brother Bob and sisters Nancy and Jill also went to Stevens Grade School. We lived across the street from Chief Garry Park on East Mission. We had a lot of family picnics there and played baseball and football at the park, a great place to grow up. At the Fox Theater I watched an exciting movie called 'Wings.' It was the story of World War I aviation and showed fighters twisting and turning in dog fights that I remember vividly.

One day there was a great sadness; adults were crying. "President Roosevelt has died," I was told. Several months later there was great rejoicing, and horns began honking all over town celebrating the end of World War II.

The happiest and best times I remember as a boy were the summers I spent at my grandfather's cabin in northern Idaho on beautiful Lake Coeur d'Alene. For me the cabin, built shortly after the war ended, was an escape from the civilized world as I knew it, namely boring school and pesky adults always trying to tell me what to do and when to do it.

Grandfather wasn't like most adults. Born in Sweden in the late 1800s, William C. Rydblom was a tall, handsome man who drew his share of friendly looks from the ladies. Better yet, he was my pal and best friend and let me have the freedom to develop and be myself in that outdoor environment. He bought me a canvas-covered duck boat, powered by an old three-horsepower Johnson outboard, which gave me the freedom to explore the lake on my own. Trolling for cutthroat trout with my grandfather, exploring the surrounding forests with his dog Butch, and swimming in the lake, I developed a deep love and appreciation for nature.

One of my favorite places was a secret marsh across the lake south of Harrison, where I caught large bullfrogs. They were delicious; of course, you had to pull out the cords in their legs or they would start jumping around in the frying pan.

The summer following my freshman year at Northwest Christian High School, four of us boys, Lee McLaughlin, Ben Mitchell, Jim Goerz and I, all classmates, and our coach whom we fondly called "Chops," and his wife drove in the Bowdy's station wagon from Spokane to Olympic National Park on the Washington coast. My best friend Jim Goerz and I camped together. We all backpacked deep into the old growth rain forest, hiking 13 miles into Enchanted Valley, where an old hunting lodge stood surrounded by magnificent waterfalls. Mr. Bowdy led a devotion by a creek. He was a wonderful Christian man and role model I looked up to.

We saw black bears and large, magnificent Roosevelt elk along the trail. We backpacked, netted smelt in the Pacific surf, dug clams, and spent time at a massive lodge overlooking the incredibly beautiful Lake Quinault; the seeds were planted that one day would take us to the far north and a different way of life. That camping trip was the highlight of my years at Northwest Christian High School. Mrs. Bowdy said years later after Bob, her husband, died, that the camping trip was the highlight of their years teaching at Northwest Christian High School!

That fall when we returned to school as sophomores, Jim and I began meeting secretly. Our guide was a book called *How to Live in the Woods on $10 a Week*, by Bradford Angier. We made plans to run away, slip across the border into Canada and live the lives of mountain men.

We didn't run away, but we kept in touch through the years and kept the dream alive. In 1955 at age 17 while a junior at Northwest Christian High School in Spokane I enlisted in the United States Navel Reserve for a six-year program, two years of active duty and four years of Reserves, with my high school buddy, Gary Johnson. I was honorably discharged in 1961. Gary spent 30 years in the Navy and retired as a Lt. Commander.

After graduation from high school I went to San Diego for Navy Boot Camp and then flew to Hickam Air Force Base in Hawaii in a Lockheed Constellation (Connie), a unique four-engine propeller plane that had three vertical tails. When we landed at Hickam Air Force Base at 0300 I got off the plane and felt that warm tropical breeze for the first time. That was my first airplane ride, and I thoroughly enjoyed it!

After catching a ride to Pearl Harbor I met my home for the next two years, the Fleet Oil Tanker USS Hassayampa AO-145! As I walked aboard the ship, I saluted the officer of the deck and said "permission to come aboard ship, sir!" He saluted back and said, "permission granted." Pearl Harbor was our home port. I became a storekeeper, after I taught myself to type 35 words a minute, and got out of the deck crew where I chipped paint and painted, swabbed the deck and threw garbage over the fantail (stern of the ship).

One of my fun jobs was being a duty driver and driving our Captain around in the ship's newer Chevy, and the crew in our Jeep. Another cool job I had was I manned the annunciators (port and starboard throttles) when we left a port and entered a port. I had my hands on both throttles, and when the pilot gave me a command. I repeated the order and moved the throttles to the correct position.

We spent six months in Hawaii water and six months in between the Philippines and Japan (during the winter months) refueling the fleet. We would be fueling one carrier on the starboard side and one destroyer on the port side at the same time.

After completing my two years of active duty I caught a troop transport ship in the Philippines and headed for the Navy Base, Treasure Island at San Francisco to get released from the two years of active duty. On April 2, 1958, my 20th birthday, in the middle of the Pacific Ocean on the troop ship, I was thinking about my immediate plans once I became a civilian again in a few days. I'm a Christian, and I prayed that God would give me a son! I accepted Jesus Christ as my Lord and Savior when I was in grade school. This was an exciting time and soon those youthful dreams of going to the far north to build a log cabin, fish, hunt and living off the land, could be fulfilled.

While I was in the Philippines on board my ship, I read a book about a couple that bought their own plane, so I decided I would get a plane. But first I would have to learn how to fly.

After getting released from active duty at Treasure Island, I caught a bus to Spokane to visit my parents before heading north, where I intended to live out my life. My worldly possessions consisted of a new 270 Winchester rifle, a new 12-gauge Winchester shotgun, navy clothes, pictures and a map of where I planned to live!

Following a short visit with my parents, I decided to meet the young lady who had written me a few letters while I was overseas. She had obtained my address from a high school girlfriend. After a thirty-minute drive to nearby Rathdrum, Idaho, I pulled into the Park Ranch. I stepped out of the car and saw a young woman on horseback galloping across the meadow, her long black hair flowing in the breeze. By the time she dismounted in front of me, I was already a goner. I promptly fell in love with this young beauty, Kathryn Park, and my trek north was put on hold. Kathy was going to college and living with her parents.

We shared a dream together of one day having a son and a log cabin in the far north. I became a logger, working at Burke, Idaho in the summer, where I set chokers on a high line off an Idaho jammer. In no time I was rid of my two years of Navy flab. I later set chokers behind a Cat north of Spokane during the winter months.

Kathryn and I were married February 18, 1959. We spent our honeymoon on Lake Coeur d'Alene at Grandpa's cabin. The following spring we camped out, working our way into Montana, where we got a job on a lookout station for the Hungry Horse Ranger District. The supervising ranger was Dick Baldwin, a super nice guy. As I gazed into the Rocky Mountains, I wondered how long it would be until we went north. Glacier Park was several miles north of our lookout. We spotted several fires from Desert Lookout and earned our keep that summer. After Kathy fixed our breakfast of sourdough pancakes, she would vomit over the railing. She had morning sickness and was expecting our baby around the first of the year. While looking for fires I became fascinated with the raw, rugged beauty of the Rocky Mountains and they became my favorite mountains.

We had several encounters with black bears. One came walking up the steps to the top of the lookout around lunchtime, planning to help himself to our screened cooler just outside the door. We chased him off. Another bear and I went around and around in a circle – I had an axe, but the bear wasn't the least bit intimidated, although he finally left in disgust without getting his fill in our garbage pit. Kathy grew up in the country and loved the outdoors and riding her horse. She never complained, living without plumbing or electricity.

On January 25, 1960, a cold winter's day during a snow storm I was working for FK&L Lumber Company at Martin City, Montana on the Green Chain stacking lumber when I got a call that Kathy's water had broken while she was putting out a chimney fire. I raced home and got stuck in our driveway in deep snow. I borrowed the neighbor's car, and we raced down the highway some 30 miles to the Kalispell County Hospital in Kalispell, Montana. Kathy kept saying, "Pull over; I'm having the baby," and I kept saying we were almost there. Five minutes after arriving at the hospital, our son William Scott Whitesitt, who is the joy of our lives, was born! God answered my prayer to have a son. My favorite Bible verse is John 3:16.

The following summer I began flight training at the Kalispell County Airport with Jack Archibald in his two-place fabric-covered taildragger (a plane with a tail wheel), a Taylor Craft N44286 equipped with a 65-horsepower Continental engine. We practiced stalls, emergency landings, turns, climbs, descents, landings and takeoffs for some ten hours. I was working for the forest Service at the Hungry Horse Ranger Station for the season. Jack was flying Forestry Patrol in his Cessna 180.

Late one quiet afternoon on September 25, 1960 after we landed he said, "Stop and let me out. Take her up, Larry, and make three landings. She's all yours," and he stepped out of the right side of the plane and walked away from the runway. I was about to make my first solo flight.

Full power on the throttle without Jack's weight made a remarkable difference, and my craft responded quickly. Forward pressure on the elevator control lifted the tail wheel, and with slight back pressure on the elevators my craft quickly left the earth and climbed to the circuit altitude of 1,000 feet. Looking over at the empty seat made me realize it was just the two of us, my craft and I, as we soared through the clear Montana skies in the heart of the Rockies.

Flying abreast of the end of the west runway, I reduced the throttle and began my descent, turning base when I was about 45 degrees from the end of the runway and then another turn to final. Floating down in this high-lift, high-wing airplane, it soared as if I were in a glider. Rounding out above the numbers and continuing back pressure on the elevator control to the three-point landing attitude (stalling the airplane), my craft decided to float – and float for quite some distance – until it was ready to touch down. It did so very gently to a three-point landing. After two more landings I taxied back to the tie downs, but it was quite some time before my head came out of the clouds. What could be more exciting and important than to pilot a plane alone? I made most landings in a taildragger in the three-point configurative (all three wheels touching at the same time); however, I occasionally made wheel landings on the main gear. Shortly after my solo flight we returned to Spokane, Washington.

One memorable forest fire I fought was in the Bob Marshall Wilderness area. We hiked in 18 miles and relieved smoke jumpers who had parachuted in and put a ring about the fire. Hot food and supplies were parachuted in to our camp on a Beech 18 plane. We had experimental paper sleeping bags that had to be doubled up to keep us warm. We worked 12 hours a day on the fire with water packs on our backs that we sprayed on the fire as well as using a Polansky tool to dig and mix up dirt with the fire to put it out. One day coming off the fire to our sleeping bags, we found them covered with syrup dropped from a parachute that hit a tree above our sleeping bags.

We purchased our first plane, a two-place Piper J-3 Cub (a taildragger), at Felts Field for $900.00 when Scott was about two months old. It had no electrical system, so I had to hand-crank the propeller to start the engine. I had about 20 flying hours and a student pilot license, which meant I couldn't take up passengers. We built a grass airstrip at Kathy's parents' home, which had 400 acres and was located 1-1/2 miles north of Rathdrum, Idaho. It was a short strip, but I always flew solo, so the Cub was light and got in the air quickly, giving me enough room to take off safely, and it was good practice. I didn't have to worry about other planes. We kept our plane at Felts Field in Spokane, flying from there to our grass strip was about 30 miles. Flying above the highway from Felts, I watched the cars below going about the same speed as my plane. Being able to experience the marvel of flight in my own plane was a dream come true.

My brother-in-law, Jim Stevens, was a flight instructor at Felts Field for Mammer & Schreck Flying Service. Jim was a skydiver and decided to take up three men who wanted to become skydivers. They climbed aboard a Cessna 172 on our strip for their first lesson. I talked to one of the men several years later named John. He told me that at one time, he decided to become a skydiver! He said, "I got in the airplane by Rathdrum for my lesson, and as we went down the runway I noticed the grass getting longer and longer, and then we crashed off the end of the runway," (that is about a 10-foot drop-off) "and I never took another lesson!" I said, "John, that was my brother-in-law, Jim Stevens."

The Cessna 172 is a safe airplane, but with a small engine (145 hp), it needs a longer runway. Jim was married to Kathy's sister, Dolores. Jim went on to fly for an airline. One day he took a student up for a helicopter lesson, and because of a mechanical failure it crashed, and Jim was killed.

We sold our Piper J-3 Cub and I got my private pilot's license on October 5, 1961 at Felts Field. When Scott was 18 months old Kathy, Scott and I flew in a Cessna 150 from Felts Field to Radium Hot Springs in British Columbia for two days of soaking and enjoying the beautiful scenery. On the flight back to Felts Field we hit some rough turbulence, but Scott just laughed and thought it great fun to bounce around the sky.

When Scott was 1-1/2 years old we manned Faucett Lookout in the Coeur d'Alene National Forest. Our perch overlooked Pend Oreille Lake. One day Scott disappeared. I called our faithful German shepherd, Smoky, and said, "Smoky, go find Scott." He cocked his head up at me for a moment, about-faced to the west, and led us in a direct line through thick bush to our son. Tears were streaming down Scott's dirty face and, as he raised his arms, I reached down and picked him up for a mutual, grateful bear hug. The relief and joy of finding him safe was overwhelming. Kathy was a wonderful mother, and she and Scott were always close.

That was a special summer for all of us as we lived together 24 hours a day and became very close. We lived in a small one-room building with lots of windows on the ground and climbed up a high steel tower to the lookout. We built a fence around the bottom to keep Scott from climbing it. The morning after the first snowfall, deer came up close to look through the window at us. That first snow ended our lookout days, and we boarded up the windows and headed down the mountain in our blue 1953 Chevy.

In the spring of 1964, Kathy and our four-year-old son Scott and I immigrated to Canada. We pulled a trailer with our worldly possessions behind our 1953 blue Chevy. On the way out of Spokane we stopped to say goodbye to our friends, Mr. and Mrs. Bard, whose daughter Lois gave Kathy my address in the Navy. We never forgot what Scott said: "Dad, we better hurry or we'll be late for Canada."

After leaving Spokane, we drove to Seattle and met up with my high school buddy, Jim Goerz, his wife Mardella and their children, Laury and Brent. Jim was driving a Jeep pickup and pulling a large trailer with their possessions. We crossed the border at Blaine, Washington and became landed immigrants. I kissed the ground. At last Jim and I were fulfilling our high school dreams of going north to build a log cabin, fish, hunt and live off the land in a wilderness area. It just took us longer than planned!

Jim and his family purchased land near Smithers, British Columbia and built their log home there. Kathy, Scott and I drove about 30 miles north and built a one-room cabin along the Kispiox River. I helped build a sawmill and worked there until they went out of business. Then I was without a job. I shot a moose and a mountain goat and caught a lot of Coho salmon in the river, and we lived off the land. We had no electricity, and with two buckets got our water out of the Kispiox River. In the winter we had to cut a hole in the ice to get water. The outhouse was mighty cold at -30 degrees. Scott caught a nice dolly varden about two pounds with a wide happy smile. He got his first dog in Canada, a German shepherd pup we called Gretchen at the cabin. The Kispiox River was noted for world record steelhead, so we often saw fishermen along the river.

Kathy was a good pioneer wife and never once complained about not having indoor plumbing or electricity. We had a wood cook stove and a wood heater made out of a 45-gallon drum. The legs were made out of chain link welded together.

We moved to Lowell Davidson Ranch about 10 miles north of Smithers, British Columbia and took care of it. Our dog, Gretchen, was poisoned and we lost her. She had a litter of pups, and we kept one female, which we named after her mother, "Gretchen." The Davidson family were really nice friends.

In 1966 I was a logger, falling large coastal timber near Terrace, British Columbia with a power saw. One day a limb fell on my hard hat, knocking me to the ground. As I lay stretched out on the ground, a de Havilland Beaver float plane flew low overhead. Looking at that Beaver, I decided to change occupations, as it looked like a lot safer job and a more enjoyable occupation. I picked up my bones, told my boss, "I quit," and never logged again. The New York Times did a study of the 18 most dangerous jobs, and the most dangerous job was logging, the second most dangerous jobs were pilots and aircrews. The article was in the business section Friday, March 20, 2015.

We sold our plane, an Aroneca Chief, a two-place taildragger, and I began taking flying lessons at Caribou Air Charter at Kelowna, British Columbia. In the spring of 1967 I obtained my Canada Commercial Pilot License and Flight Instructor's rating.

On June 5, 1967 I was hired as a commercial pilot by Bill Harrison, owner of Omineca Air Service at McLure Lake near Smithers, British Columbia. I made my first flight that same day with Carl Faye. We flew a Piper Super Cub floatplane to Alice Arm, an inlet of the Pacific Ocean. It was hard to believe I was being paid to do something I loved, flying a floatplane. I flew the Super Cub Cessna 185 and Beaver float planes in the summer and skis in the winter. We never flew wheel planes.

We purchased ten treed acres a few miles east of Smithers, British Columbia in 1968 and hired Ted Strand to build us a log cabin like they do in Norway where he was from. He told me to fell the trees in the fall when the sap was low and then the logs wouldn't crack much. In the fall I fell about 50 trees. I put them on stringers off the ground for winter. I used a spud and draw knife to peel the logs. Ted constructed the log cabin without any chinking between the logs! He scribed the logs and used an axe to concave each log to fit the log below it to fit perfectly with only a strip of insulation between the logs. After 15 years the log cabin was tight, and the logs still fit perfectly.

Tommy Walker, a big game outfitter and guide in northern British Columbia whom I flew for saw my log cabin and had Ted Strand build him a log cabin. Ted liked the area and moved there by a lake, where he could hunt and live his free lifestyle in the wilderness.

One day in the Cessna 185 floatplane I landed on the lake where Ted lived, which was near Dease Lake, British Columbia. Ted said he would like to fly over to see a pack of young wolves that Gordon Eastman (a photographer for Walt Disney movies) was raising for a movie. I flew Ted to the lake where the wolves were, and we had a nice visit. That was the last time I saw this remarkable log cabin builder who was a mountain man. One day Ted and his dog were hunting mountain sheep in the snow and were buried in an avalanche. Wilbur O'Brien, a helicopter pilot who managed the base at Dease Lake, flew Ted's body out when the snow melted in the spring.

On April 8, 1969 my high school buddy Jim Goerz, who immigrated to Canada with me, was in the right co-pilot seat as I flew Omineca's Cessna 185 ski plane CF-OXE. We flew to a wilderness trading post at the Indian village of Takla Post, B.C. located on the east side of Takla Lake with some freight. We made a normal approach, but shortly after touchdown the right landing gear on Jim's side broke, and we skidded in a half circle on the frozen lake. The right wing and prop were bent, and we were covered with gas from the wing tank. I yelled, "Run, Jim!" as we climbed out on the ice, fearing fire, as the engine was hot. We stopped a good distance away, but the plane didn't catch on fire.

On inspection by our aviation engineer, he discovered a crack on a supportive component of the landing gear that caused the structural break – it was no one's fault! During the 52-year period I flew, this was the only accident I had! I had my share of close calls, but I believe God was looking after me.

Larry flying his favorite plane, The Red Beaver float plane CF-IBP off the South Nahannie River, Northwest Territories in the 1970's

Old Crow Indian carrying fresh killed moose and salmon to the village from the Porcupine River.

Old Crow, Yukon. Boats on the banks of the Porcupine River in front of the village, September 5th, 1989. Larry landed on the village airstrip and spent two days here. He also flew to the Inuit town of Tuktoyaktuk, Northwest Territories on September 3, 1989 located on the Arctic Ocean for a two day visit. Larry flew from Felts Field, Spokane, Washington alone in a Cessna 172 for his first visit to the Arctic Ocean.

Allen Benjamin with one of his perfectly matched Siberian Husky sled dogs that he raised at Old Crow. He races his dogs in winter at Whitehorse, the capitol of the Yukon. Allen proudly talks about his sled dogs.

Caribou on a snow field, Northwest Territories. About 180,000 caribou, called the Porcupine Caribou herd migrate near Old Crow in the spring on their way to Alaska to calf and return to the Yukon and Northwest Territories in the fall.

Larry Whitesitt with his father, Valmur, who was a trucker all of his life with a load of logs. Larry wanted to become a logger some day!

The Whitesitt family. Father Valmur holding Robert (Bob), Mother Jeanne holding Nancy and Larry standing, on E. 1404 Mallon, Spokane, Washington, at our grandparents on mom's side, Esther and William Rydbloms home.

Grandfather William Charles Rydblom standing behind his father, Edward and his mother Ingeborg. Grandpa was born in Sweden in 1888 and came to the United States when he was about 4 years old. Mother was his first child, I was his first grandson, and my son, William Scott Whitesitt, who we named after Grandpa, was his first great-grandchild. The happiest days of my boyhood were spent with Grandpa at his cabin on beautiful Lake Coeur d'Alene. He was my fishing pal and my best friend.

Larry's grandparents on his mother's side. Ester and William C. Rydblom.
They were wonderful grandparents who spoiled me in so many ways. We
were very close.

Larry Whitesitt sitting on Grandpa Rydblom's lap by Lake Pend Oreille in 1938.

Grandfather William C. Rydblom and Larry at Grandpa's home in Spokane, Washington, 1942

Larry in the duck boat in Lake Coeur d'Alene—Harrison, Idaho is in the background. Grandpa Rydblom bought this boat for Larry and with a 3 HP Johnson outboard which gave him the freedom to explore the lake on his own.

War years, 1943 – Aunt JoAnn and her brother—Uncle Bill Rydblom Jr. in Coast Guard uniform, He was my boyhood hero! Spokane, Washington.

Larry Whitesitt in back. Sisters, Jill, Nancy, and brother Bob in front at 1404 E. Mallon. Grandparents Ester and Bill Rydblom's home.

Jim Goerz in front, Ben Mitchell, Larry Whitesitt, Lee McLaughlin, and our coach Mr. Bowdy and his dog. We are backpacking 13 miles to Enchanted Valley.

Enchanted Valley in Olympic Natural Park is surrounded by beautiful waterfalls. We stayed at this deserted hunting lodge overnight. We saw Rooseveldt Elk and Black bears along the hiking trail.

The USS Hassayampa AO-145, a navy fleet oil tanker that Larry served on from 1956 to 1958. Our home port was Pearl Harbor, Hawaii.

Larry Whitesitt on the right and a fellow sailor on the left on our ship USS Hassayampa AO-145 in the vast Pacific Ocean.

On September 25, 1960 Larry soloed in this Taylor Craft N44286 equipped
with a 65hp Continental engine at the Kalispell County Airport in
Montana. Jack Archibald, standing by the plane, was an excellent instructor
and a super nice guy who taught me to fly in this plane he owns.

Our first plane. A Piper J-3 Cub N42200 with a 65hp Continental Engine.
We purchased it in February 1961 for $900 at Felts Field. Larry, Kathy
holding Scott (a future pilot) and cousin Danny in the cockpit, at our grass
strip at Rathdrum, Idaho that we called "Park International Airport."

Left: Helen Park, Kathy's sister,, Kathy Whitesitt, Larry Whitesitt, and brother Bob Whitesitt "Best Man." at our wedding, February 18, 1959.

Desert Lookout, our home in summer of 1959. My sister Jill Whitesitt by the tent, on a visit with mom and dad. We worked for the Hungry Horse Ranger District in Montana and spotted many fires and earned our keep. My sister Jill died of Lupus at age 13. She was a beautiful girl and wonderful sister, full of life who died too young.

Larry Whitesitt standing by the storage log building at Faucett Lookout in the summer of 1961.

After the summer on Faucett Lookout. Kathy, Scott, Larry and our dog, Smokey, went down the Oregon Coast and into California for part of the winter.

Faucett Lookout, Coeur d'Alene National Forest 1961. Scott was 1-1/2 years old when Kathy and Larry manned the lookout above Pend Oreille Lake in Idaho.

Scott Whitesitt and his dog, Smokey, at Faucett Lookout summer 1961. Scott got lost and we said, "Smokey, find Scott," and he led us to our boy who was crying with tears streaking his dirty face. I knelt down and we gave each other a big wonderful bear hug. So glad he was safe.

Scott at Knott's Berry Farm in California just after Christmas.
We rode this train and some masked robber's came aboard. Scott
had his cap gun that he received for Christmas. He pulled his
gun out of his holster and pointed it at the robbers to protect us!

This is Larry's first airplane, a Piper J-3 Cub N42200, which he purchased
fo $900 in the fall of 1961 when he had a total of 15 hours flying experience.
This picture was taken north of the Alaska range.

Laury and Brent Goerz and Scott Whitesitt sitting on Larry's 1953 Blue Chevy, headed north in British Columbia, as landed immigrants, spring of 1964 to fulfill our youthful dream of building a log cabin in the wilderness, fishing, hunting, and living off the land and become a bush pilot.

Our simple cabin we built along the Kispiox River in northern British Columbia, We fished, hunted and lived off the land, 1964-1965.

Ted Strand, our builder on top of log wall—Larry, Kathy and Scott
Whitesitt's log cabin was constructed in 1968, about 8 miles east of
Smithers, British Columbia

Our log cabin completed. Left, Uncle Jess McDaniel, father Valmur
Whitesitt, Larry, Kathy, Scott and our dog Gretchen. Summer of 1968.

Scott and Larry's family reunion in Spokane July 25, 1969. Back row: Bob
Whitesitt, Nancy & Doug Furlott, Dennis & JoAnn McDaniel, Jeanne
& Val Whitesitt, Sue Clark, Larry. Front row: Jess McDaniel, Danny
McDaniel, Jan McDaniel, Scott Whitesitt, Jon Furlott and Kenny Clark.
Larry left Spokane on August 2nd driving to Watson Lake, Yukon and
arriving August 5, 1969 to begin flying for B.C. Yukon Air Service. This
was Larry's first time in Canada's Yukon Territory and the fulfillment of a
boyhood dream, to go to the Yukon after reading Jack London's *The Call of
the Wild*.

Scott Whitesitt and his faithful dog, Gretchen, by the igloo Scott made and slept in with his dog beside our log cabin. They were great pals.

Larry flew his family in this Cessna 185 CF-OXE into the wilderness at Kitchner Lake, BC, in 1968. Left, father Valmur, mother Jeanne, Kathy, and Scott. We caught nice 2-4 pound trout.

Larry Whitesitt standing beside the Beaver Ski-Plane CF-JOS in March 1968 on the frozen Finlay River at Ft. Ware, BC while flying a charter for IPEC. We stayed overnight with Art Van Sommers a legendary river boat man that ran a trading post here at the Indian Village. In the winter while flying ski planes I saw large packs of wolves: they are one of my favorite wild animals! Once I landed at a trapper's cabin in Northern BC with a Beaver on skis when it was -60 degrees.

Larry Whitesitt standing by the wrecked Cessna 185 Ski-Plane CF-OXE. Jim Goerz was along for the ride and it was a wild one. I was flying freight for the fur trader Jack Newcomb who ran a trading post for the Indians at Takla Post, BC when the right landing gear collapsed. It was a structural failure and no one's fault. This is the only accident Larry had during the 52 years he flew. About 20% of the pilots he flew with were killed mostly because of bad weather. Larry had his share of close calls and believes God was looking out for him.

ARCTIC OCEAN

TUKTOYAKTUK
ALASKA
YUKON
DAWSON
WHITEHORSE
ATLIN
FRANCES
LK.
WATSON
LK.
SCOOP LK.
FT. BABINE
McCLURE LK.
BRITISH
COLUMBIA
SPOKANE, WA

MACKENZIE RIVER
MACKENZIE MTNS
FT. SIMPSON
ROCKY MTNS.

NORMAN WELLS
HEADLESS VALLEY
YELLOWKNIFE

NORTHWEST TERRITORIES

ARCTIC CIRCLE

ALBERTA
SASKATCHEWAN
CANADA
USA

MANITOBA

HUDSON BAY

ONTARIO

QUEBEC

Chapter 2

YUKON FLYING ADVENTURE BEGINS

Work was slow, and we had too many pilots for the work available in the summer of 1969, so we got in very few hours flying. In the middle of July I drove to Bill Harrison's home and gave him my two weeks' notice. I planned to go to Seattle for an instrument rating so I could fly for Interior Airways in Alaska on a Hercules aircraft. An Interior Airways pilot had told me my chances of going to work for them would be good if I had an instrument rating.

A few days later Grant Luck, the working base manager, offered me an attractive salary to go to work at B.C. Yukon Air Service of Watson Lake for the remainder of the season. With little hesitation, I accepted. I had requested a transfer earlier to do this, but they had wanted me to stay at Maclure Lake.

Scott and I departed Smithers for Spokane, arriving on July 25th. Scott was to stay at Grandma and Grandpa Whitesitt's. August 2nd I left Spokane in my VW on course to Watson Lake, Yukon Territory. During the long, dusty and muddy drive up the Alaska Highway my windshield broke, but I arrived at last at Watson Lake. I drove several miles past it, not believing the few sparse buildings were my destination. It was the 5th of August. I turned north at Watson Lake and drove another six miles to B.C. Yukon Float Base. I was finally here and ready to begin my first flight in the Yukon.

At last, those boyhood dreams, after reading Jack London's *The Call of the Wild* and listening on the radio to Sergeant Preston of the Northwest Mounted Police, to go to the Yukon happened today, August 5, 1969. Now my youthful dreams of going to the far north, building a log cabin, having a son, fishing, hunting, living off the land and today beginning my life as a Yukon bush pilot have been fulfilled above and beyond my wildest imagination!

After my long trek to Watson Lake, I really appreciated the vastness and the remoteness of this land. Being basically a loner with a love for the wilderness, I felt a closeness, a kinship, at home here in the Yukon.

I flew with a fellow by the name of Jim Thibaudeau longer than any other pilot, from 1969 to 1975. The first time I met Jim was at B.C. Yukon's seaplane base in 1969. Jim's friendly grin, warm Yukon welcome and handshake greeted me as I walked through the door. It was the beginning of my Yukon adventure, and I was to get well acquainted over the years with this bush pilot.

Jim was about 25 years old, 5 feet 10 inches, with a trim, well-built body. He was a handsome man, and I noticed that women gave him more than an occasional glance and made complimentary remarks among themselves about his good looks. He wore cowboy boots, blue jeans, a blue shirt and an Air Force flight jacket. Jim had a good touch and feel for an airplane, and you knew right away he was in control. He was the kind of bush pilot that Hollywood would portray and, in fact, he did some flying for several films. He lived with one filmmaker for a year or so and flew his Super Cub, making a movie about a bush pilot who crashed in the wilderness. He also flew Watson Lake Flying Service's red Beaver CF-IBP in a film depicting a true story about a man and a woman from Alaska who crashed near Aeroplane Lake, 80 miles south of Watson Lake and just west of the Rocky Mountains. This couple survived longer without food than anyone ever has in the wilderness.

Jim and I each flew Beavers for B.C. Yukon. His was one of the best performing Beavers in the country, and he was proud of his plane. The following year Jim went to work for Watson Lake Flying Service, and I flew his favorite plane that year.

Jim was sweet on a girl named Lynn, a cute bank teller. She was totally taken by this handsome Yukon pilot. One memorable night there was a party at the seaplane office. The northern lights were brightly rippling across the sky like giant colored curtains, and Jim said that some nights when it was cold you could hear the northern lights. Jim and Lynn got into a friendly wrestling match, and Jim ended up on top.

This was my first season in the Yukon. I felt that at last I was seeing the real North and was beginning to feel at home in this vast, spectacular country of my boyhood dreams.

Ernie Harrison was my boss when I arrived. He was a man in his 40s, of medium height and very friendly. He gave me my first flight the day I arrived. Ernie's open, friendly manner and experience as a bush pilot were well known in these parts. He was half owner of B.C. Yukon Air Service, and his cousin Bill Harrison, my former boss and owner of Omineca Air Service owned the other half of the company.

Shortly after arriving in Watson Lake, Ernie Harrison said, "Larry, you have a trip to Moodie Lake a hundred miles south in the Rocky Mountain Trench for Frank Cooke." I was to take B.C. Yukon's Beaver CF-JBP and fly some freight to Moodie Lake in northern British Columbia.

It was August 10, 1969, and this was my first trip to this area, so I had my sectional maps on my lap. The weather was lousy after takeoff, and I had to climb over the cloud cover, but I could see holes in the layers. I was flying, feeling good and following a river when I noticed the river was running the wrong direction, according to the map. I discovered I was not sure of my location. In other words, I was lost!

A short time later, I saw a lake through a hole in the clouds and thought I spotted a couple of pack dogs by a cabin. This made me feel better; I could land and ask directions. Upon landing, I taxied the Beaver to shore, tied up and proceeded to climb up the bank, intending to walk over to the cabin. As I topped the bank I met a large mass of fur coming toward me only 15 feet away. I froze. The grizzly didn't like my looks any better than I liked his. I walked slowly backward to the plane, and he went the other direction, much to my relief. Looking at my map, I figured I was probably at Scoop Lake. Moodie Lake was about 15 miles southwest.

I flew on to Moodie Lake and met Frank Cooke for the first time. Frank, a lean six-footer who looked like a cowboy – which he was – had wrangled horses since his childhood. He was a nice looking, intelligent individual, friendly, well organized and seemed completely in charge of every situation. I explained my encounter with the bear and asked, "Frank, are there any pack dogs by the cabin?"

He replied, "No, but I'll bet they were bears, and they probably wrecked my cabin." Frank rounded up a hunter, and we flew back to Scoop Lake to deal with the grizzlies.

Frank describes this event: "I remember it like it was yesterday, and it was the first time we met. You flew in and asked me if there were big dogs or some other animals down at Scoop Lake, and I said there shouldn't be, and no people either. Having lived in the north for so long, I thought there had to be a bear fooling around. I also knew in my mind that they would smash a window and get in my cookhouse and wreck everything, which is exactly what they did. I asked the hunter if he wanted to have some fun, and he said, 'Doing what?' When I explained it to him, he became excited and said, 'How can we get down there?' I told him I would hire you to fly us down to Scoop Lake to take a look, and then we would fly back to Moodie Lake. So I chartered the Beaver, and away we went.

"When we tied up at Scoop Lake I remember looking out the window of the Beaver, and sure enough, there was one grizzly in the yard. I wasn't going to let the hunter shoot him, but I looked over at the cookhouse door and saw that it was open and all the windows were knocked out and knew there would be a mess in the cabin. The bear started to run, and I said, 'Shoot him!' He did and killed him. The gun had no sooner gone off when out the door came another grizzly, and then out the window another. I hated to shoot them, but I knew I had to, as they would never leave and are very destructive. One started down the lake, but the other one started toward us at the lakeshore by the plane.

"I said to the hunter, 'You take the one going down the lake, and I'll take the one heading for us,' as he was close, and I wasn't sure how good he could shoot. I don't like being in too close to a grizzly with a strange hunter in case he wounds him; grizzlies can be very dangerous at close quarters. I knew my gun and knew I could kill with one shot, and I did. He shot, and – sure enough! – He wounded his bear. I walked over to the dead one and then finished off the one he had wounded. I can't remember his name, but he sure was excited. He had never seen or participated in that kind of event. It was just another day to me; I have seen lots of these real dangerous situations in my life."

I sat down on one of the bunks to write out a flight ticket. My pants suddenly became very damp, and a strong odor penetrated the air. The bears had urinated on the mattress and, confined in the warm cockpit of the Beaver, I had to endure this odor all the way back to Watson Lake.

Frank reminisced, "I remember one evening at Moodie Lake, there were 20 of us having a big barbecue in front of the cabins on the lake. I had a big black work dog called Zero at the camp to warn me if anything was around. We had a big fire going, and it was just starting to get dark. Everybody was singing and having a few drinks, but I always kept my eyes peeled for anything wrong, since that was my job, and I always kept my gun handy. It was my responsibility to see that nobody got hurt or got into bad situations. I looked over at the dog, and he stood up and looked up the trail going around the lake. He growled, and the hair stood up all over his back. He was a great dog! I picked up my rifle, told the women and kids to go into the cookhouse quick! I knew there was something coming down the trail. I told the hunters to get their rifles, and they thought I was kidding. Frankie and Terry knew I wasn't, so they got their guns. Sure enough, out of the edge of the clearing came five grizzlies, just like they owned the place.

"The big bear charged, and I shot it right in the mouth. When it went down, it hollered, and the rest charged. I yelled, 'Kill them,' and we did. One bear pretty near got Mac Cooke, who was only 15 years old at the time. I didn't see Mac behind me when one bear came in sideways toward me. Mac hollered, 'Look out, Dad!' It was pretty dark, and I swung around and shot him not two feet from me. When I looked around, Mac was out in the lake in water up to his waist. Everything was all over in a matter of two to three minutes, and the women and kids all came down to look. We all had a laugh at young Mac, but it was a good lesson to a lot of people, including Mac, especially for him to remember in his guiding in later years.

"All main camps should have a good, proven dog around. He is worth his grub to look after the camp. I saw a bull moose kill an Indian guide when I was a young boy on the middle river out of Fort Saint James, B.C. I have a great respect for a bull moose in a fight, more than I have for a grizzly bear, as a moose fears nothing during breeding season and will kill you quick in the right kind of situation. Even chopping wood to make a campfire will at times bring him right on the run, and he is very fast and dangerous, especially if he has been fighting and is hurt. He will charge through the camp at night. In good moose country during rutting season I always put my camp in heavy timber so the moose can't tear it apart. If he does come in, you can get behind a tree. Out in the open you have no place to go, and if you have to get your gun, you are helpless. Skook Davidson taught me as a young boy to always know where my gun was, and to put it where I can get to it quickly. It is not a case of being scared; it is a case of self-preservation and caution.

"As an outfitter or guide it is your job to look after people and to see that they are never put into bad situations, as most people and hunters you take out are from cities and just don't understand what can happen. All young guides should have to take a course and be taught how to handle people and what people expect of them, as every person who comes to your camp has a different personality. It is your job to talk to them all separately before you leave on a hunt so you know who needs more attention. I blame our own B.C. government for not making this mandatory. If it were done, then our game department would eliminate over 80 percent of their problems that are created by dumb guides, especially drinking among the help and things like that. The outfitter should have to make out a report to the Game Department on every assistant guide at the end of every season regarding that guide's progress, and then they could assess each guide. That way our guiding industry would improve dramatically, and they would know before issuing an outfitter's license if a man was capable or not. This would also give the guide an incentive to perform better, and the guiding industry would automatically improve itself. The way it is now, an outfitter can pick up any drunk off the street, buy him an assistant guide license and turn him loose with people. Customers end up spending a lot of money in Canada, and it is just a big disappointment when they go home bewildered and sad after a poor hunt. Many of them have saved a long time for a hunting trip."

Frank Cooke was born in Victoria, B.C. in 1927. He was 16 years old when he started working for Skook Davidson at his ranch on Terminus Mountain about 120 miles south of Watson Lake, along the Kechika River in the Rocky Mountain Trench.

Frank started his own guiding business in 1965 with his headquarters at Moodie Lake, B.C. 100 miles south of Watson Lake. He purchased part of Skook Davidson's guiding territory from him. He built his first main camp at Moodie Lake, and for a time his son Terry Cooke flew their own Super Cub off a rough airstrip there.

Later Frank moved his headquarters to Scoop Lake where he had a 2,000-foot airstrip built that could accommodate DC-3s and smaller aircraft. Of course, seaplanes could also land on the lake. Cabins, a cookhouse and a building with showers and indoor plumbing were built near the old cabin where we had encountered the three bears. Frank's family included his sons Frank, Jr., Terry and Mackey, his daughters Diane, Tammy, Gloria and Donna, and his wife Hattie.

Frank described his relationship with Skook Davidson, a man who was a legend in his own time: "I met Skook when I was seven years old in Fort St. James, B.C. where my father, Frank Cooke, Sr. was a provincial policeman. I used to spend all my holidays from school as a young boy helping Skook pack horses for survey parties and freighting on the Manson Trail. It was 150 miles to the mines, and we used four- and six-horse teams in the winter and big freight wagons in the summer. Skook also had 60 head of packhorses. In 1944 I left Fort St. James with Skook for the Kechika Valley with 50 packhorses, and we ended up at his home place by the end of September. We left on the 10th of May, traveling through the bush and mountains, rafting the rivers and swimming all the horses. We wintered at the home place in the Kechika

Valley and started the B.C. Yukon Boundary Survey with 40 head of packhorses, moving camps and cutting out the boundaries. That fall we drove the horses back down the highway over to Lower Post, swam the Liard and Dease Rivers, then drove our horses back to the Kechika Ranch and wintered there again. We drove our horses out the next year and worked all summer and went back and wintered there again.

"In 1948 I married Hattie at Lower Post, and I worked for Skook over all the years 'til I bought out everything west of the Kechika in 1965 and started my own big game guiding service and built up Scoop Lake from straight bush.

"I spent many a tough trip on the trail with Skook Davidson, and he obtained his first hunting party in 1947. He was the toughest, hardiest man in the bush that I ever met in my lifetime. He was very fair but very strict and could fight like a wildcat; he backed down from no one. He was born in Longside, Scotland in 1882 and came to Canada when he was 15 years old. His name was John Ogilvie Davidson. Skook was a nickname given to him by the Indians. It comes from the Indian word *Skookum*, meaning "strong," which he lived up to.

"Skook came to live in the Kechika Valley in the northern end of the Rocky Mountain Trench and established his Diamond J Ranch at the foot of Terminus Mountain in 1939. He remained there until 1972 when ill health forced him to go to the Whitehorse Hospital and then to a private hospital in Vancouver, B.C. where he died. (I remember Skook calling in on the radio, usually every day, while flying for Watson Lake Flying Service).

"Skook worked on all the big cattle ranches in the Caribou country and packed mules for old Cataline all through the Caribou gold rushes. He was a packer and freighter throughout the north 'til I met him. He went all through the First World War and was well decorated for bravery. He was a special policeman for the north while I was with him. He loved his horses and treated them like his own children. He never married or had any children.

"I knew Grant McConachie personally as a young boy. Grant's bush operation, which consisted of a Waco airplane at that time, later became Canadian Pacific Airlines. I gassed his airplanes up many a time just for a ride.

"My father, along with Russ Baker, started what became Pacific Western Airlines. Russ was operating a Junkers out of Fort St. James and later bought the first Beaver off the production line. I flew the north as a boy with them in old Fokkers, Fairchilds, Wacos, Tri Motor Fords and Norsemans. I babysat their children when they went out to dances at night and used to sit and listen to them, night after night, when they were all young men trying to get started in the flying business. My father was the only policeman north of Fort St. James, and everyone gathered at our house. My mother was a cousin of Winston Churchill, and Skook also knew him personally and drank rum with Winston during the First World War. He also went for a flight with Billy Bishop over France during the first war."

Frank was a Golden Glove boxer, and not only could he handle himself well, but he taught his sons to fight. They're all good with their fists.

During the first part of my stay at B.C. Yukon I detected some sort of conflict between Ernie and Bill Harrison. Ernie soon left Watson Lake and departed for his home at Fort St. James. Sid Baird, a partner with Bill Harrison on a helicopter venture, took charge of the base when Ernie left. Sid became my boss. Sid was one of the smoothest and most knowledgeable helicopter pilots I ever met. He had an excellent reputation in the north with clients and companies he worked for. He, Bill Harrison and some others bought Frontier Helicopters in Watson Lake and ran a very successful, safe operation in the area for many years. Sid was movie star material – extremely handsome, tall, dark-haired and broad-shouldered with a quiet nature. He was a born leader and conducted the helicopter business well. I respected and trusted this man. His wife and children lived at Watson Lake, about a block off Main Street, which is actually part of the Alaska Highway.

Jim Thibaudeau and I were living in our respective Beavers, having no place to stay. Actually it was enjoyable in some ways. The interior of the Beaver is quite large, and we could stretch out full length in our sleeping bags with foam underneath. The waves lapping against the floats at night gently rocked us to sleep. However, baths in the lake were a bit on the cold side. When Sid found out Jim and I had no place to live, he quickly obtained a room for us at the Signpost Motel in town. We shared a room and each had clean sheets and a place to shower every day. After a long day at flying, it was nice to come home to.

My first trips in a Cessna 180 were made shortly after arriving at B.C. Yukon. The Cessna 180 wasn't nearly the performer the Cessna 185 was; the engine was smaller and the load capacity was less. Most of the time, much to my delight, I flew one of the Beavers CF-JPB; it was a bush pilot's dream. Jim Thibaudeau flew the other Beaver CF-IGF, which was an exceptional performer. At that time Jim was only 25 years old and had already been flying for a few years up here.

Before we obtained a de Havilland Otter DHC-3 we used to carry some heavy loads. We counted the number of rivets under the water on the back of the floats. That would tell us how much more we could safely load aboard. We carried plywood, drill rods, boats, canoes – all these could be strapped to the floats and flown safely if they were properly tied down.

Once we got an Otter, we cut down on the Beaver's payloads. The Otter was like a big Beaver with a much greater load capacity, larger cargo doors and a much bigger hold. Bulky items fit inside, and we could eliminate a lot of external loads. The Otter carries a payload of about 2,000 pounds; the Beaver carried about 1200 pounds.

Bill Harrison hired Dennis Ball who arrived at Watson Lake in 1969 with another Otter that Bill had purchased for B.C. Yukon. Dennis had been flying back east near Lake Larounge and knew all about flying in the flat country.

We sometimes had a party at the end of a long flying day. The Yukon had the highest alcohol consumption rate in Canada, and Watson Lake had the highest rate in the Yukon.

August 13, 1969 I flew the Beaver into Dalziel's hunting camp at Bluesheep Lake in northern B.C. about 70 miles south. Dal had lived many lives, and I judged him to be in his mid 60s. He owned the oldest original building in Watson Lake, a log home. He was here in the 1930s and was the first to fly in and explore the Mackenzie Mountains extensively. He didn't say much, but I sensed he had many stories, experiences and knowledge beneath his calm exterior. His wife June was friendly and a gracious host.

Inside his log home was a fantastic trophy room. He had the second and fifth largest stone sheep in the world, fully mounted, animals from Africa, a tiger, various sheep, including one Marco Polo sheep from Afghanistan, bears, moose and other animals that he had shot.

In the early days Dal shot game and flew it into the mining camps so they could have fresh meat. He started B.C. Yukon and had one of the first Beavers in the country. He now flew a Super Cub with long-range tanks so he could keep tabs on his large hunting area and get the camps set up. Our flying service flew the hunters in and out about every ten days or so, the length of an average hunt. Dal ran a first-class operation and was well organized. In a couple of years he was to buy a completely rebuilt Beaver from Kenmore Air Harbor and fly it himself into his hunting camp.

Flying was like living in another world. Looking down and seeing shapes and forms in miniature reminded me of my size and put my problems in proper perspective. Winging over this country untouched by roads, houses or smokestacks, breathing the clean fresh air and drinking the sparkling pure water without thought of pollution brought a feeling of unmatched contentment.

Today's trip was into Little Dal Lake, named after George Dalziel, located in the rugged Mackenzie Mountains in the Northwest Territories. Four hunters, anxious to go, and their gear were on the dock. I thought to myself that it was really a pleasure to take these men into the remote areas. They had planned a year or more for this trip. Some of them had saved for years, and for some it was one hunt in a lifetime; they looked forward to thoroughly enjoying themselves.

I began the loading, putting sleeping bags and other light items in the rear and heavy things toward the front. Weight and balance were very important and could prove fatal if managed improperly. Because there was so much gear, groceries and supplies from the outfitters, I took the back seats out and soon had the gear aboard and a place on the freight for the three passengers to sit. The passenger who was to sit up front climbed in first, then the others climbed in the back. I shut the back door, shoved off from the dock and climbed into the cockpit. A shot of prime, switches on, starter engaged. The 450-horsepower Pratt & Whitney engine snorted and caught, and soon the reassuring roar drowned out all other sounds. Putting the earphones on, both to protect my hearing and at times to protect me from unwanted questions from passengers, I took off and began a shallow climbing turn to the west, circling the lake to gain altitude before heading north.

Little Dal Lake was one of my favorites. About 5600 feet above sea level, it is near the headwaters of the Redstone River and about 50 miles northeast of the South Nahanni River, some 200 miles from Watson Lake. This is tundra country. Grooves made here by tracked vehicles years ago are still visible, and the ruts get larger as the years go by. It is very fragile country; care must be exercised to keep it from being damaged by men. This is also Dall sheep country. They're the white sheep, the same that were found in Alaska. Caribou, grizzly and moose are also hunted here, but today's hunters were primarily after sheep.

Flying on a northerly heading I climbed to 8,000 feet in order to fly a straight line and maintain safety. One pass we were to fly over was over 6,000 feet, so it was nice to have altitude. Today we could fly straight over the top; other times when the weather was bad we followed valleys, sometimes several, before we could find one that was open.

Crossing the Hyland River 40 miles north we soon saw some high peaks ahead. Mount St. James MacBrien at 9,062 feet was visible. Below this peak is Glacier Lake, where I often dropped off mountain climbers who scaled this and other peaks nearby in the Mackenzie Mountains. There are some fairly extensive ice fields and glaciers around Mount St. James. The sight was awesome and sobering if you had to fly the area in bad weather.

We crossed the Yukon-Northwest Territories border about 35 miles south of the Nahanni River. We were in some of the most rugged

We made it over the Nahanni, struggling to keep flying. The plane was buffeting badly and barely flying. It was going to take bout an extra hour to get home. I was getting concerned, as we emptied two tanks and part of the remaining front one.

As we crossed into the Yukon darkness became a second concern. The light was rapidly fading. We all glanced nervously at the gas gauges, which were draining very rapidly, and it was questionable whether we would make it.

I had maintained an altitude of about 7500 feet so I could glide a good distance, and there were some lakes along the route we could land on if we had to. Finally the darker shape of Watson Lake came into view. Still maintaining lots of altitude, I began our descent. The gauge was showing empty on the front tank.

There was no moon out, and it was pitch dark as we descended over the shore of the lake. I used power and maintained a landing attitude, not able to judge distance below the tree line. We made a smooth landing and everyone, especially me, breathed a little easier.

As I looked back after landing, I thought how stupid I was trying to take everything out in one trip, but I had no idea that those caribou racks would cause such a problem. The hunter/pilots made a comment later to the outfitter about this hazardous trip, and his reply was, "Well, you made it, didn't you?"

We did make it, and I learned a good lesson. I didn't repeat that performance again. From then on, if I had to fly horns I would put only a couple outside. That way the flight characteristics were closer to normal and acceptable. I tied them on outside only if I couldn't possibly get them inside the plane.

After tying the plane down I didn't really care if I flew again, a feeling often experienced after a bad trip. However, after a good sleep, flying looks better the next day, and you know there is no other type of work that can compare. Hopefully, you learn from your mistakes or poor judgment and become a better pilot.

The last flights of the season were spooky for me. The weather was usually bad, and I wondered if I had used up my luck. I spent long days of flying and loading and unloading without any time off, maybe averaging four or five hours of sleep each day all summer.

When I woke up the morning after that last flight into Little Dal Lake, I was glad to be alive and glad that I was going south to my log home in Smithers, B.C. It was about a three-day trip, and I was anxious to get started. I enjoyed this new country, met new friends and was glad I was still in one piece. All and all, it was a memorable season, something I'd wanted to do for a long time.

When I arrived home after that long drive on the Alaska Highway, which was now mostly mud, it was good to relax with my family, catch up on what they'd been doing and sleep in my own bed. My plans were to go south to Boeing Field in Seattle to obtain a U.S. Commercial and Instrument Rating and then my Airline Transport Pilot Rating.

It was October 31, 1969, and I was just getting ready to depart Boeing Field for my first flight in a Cherokee PA-28. My instructor, Jim Gill of Galvins Flight Service, knew his job well and was an excellent pilot and good instructor.

To me it was like driving on the freeway. Airplanes were all over the sky, and I kept a wary eye out landing and taking off, but then I was under the hood learning proper instrument flight techniques. It was a whole new world as I learned to believe the gauges. The first nine hours or so were preparation for the U.S. commercial check ride, which I passed successfully November 5. Then I started the basic instrument course in earnest.

Tracking, VOR intercepts, ADF tracking, ADF approaches, ATC clearances, ILS and holding patterns swam in my head. Finally on December 31, 1969, the last day of the year, I obtained my U.S. Instrument Rating. I passed the written test earlier with good marks, thanks to an excellent teacher who made it clear and enjoyable.

Driving back to my log house in Smithers, my spirit was light. I had reached another goal and had a U.S. Commercial and Instrument Rating. It was good to be with my family again; Scott was such a fine son. We had a good time taking it easy, and we got caught up on events. I stayed home and did some cross-country skiing, but soon my restless spirit longed for the Yukon. I looked forward to returning and flying once again in the vast wilderness.

I left for Fairbanks, Alaska about the 1st of March to see about a flying job I hoped to get on with Interior Airways, flying as a crewmember on a Hercules. It was 60 degrees below zero when I got off a commercial jet at Fairbanks. I went to the office of Interior Airways to apply for a job, but they had been laying off workers and wouldn't be hiring for quite some time. The layoffs were caused by environmental concern among citizens' groups and certain government agencies regarding the North Slope oil exploration that was a big part of this company's business.

I hitchhiked a ride from Fairbanks to Watson Lake with a trucker. Along the way, we stopped at a rather seedy-looking Chinese restaurant at Whitehorse for breakfast. While eating, I noticed some dark objects in my oatmeal and quietly asked the waitress to come over to my table. She was in a dither about her relief that had not shown up for work. In an angry mood, she asked, "Well, what's wrong with you?"

"Oh, there's mouse turds in my mush." The restaurant got deathly quiet as all the patrons' ears perked up, and they contemplated their breakfasts with sober expressions. We finally got back on the Alaska Highway.

At B.C. Yukon Air Service, I talked to Grant Luck and was hired to fly with Ron Wells on Transprovincial's Otter, which was temporarily leased to B.C. Yukon. Ron, an old-time bush pilot, and I flew diesel fuel for a mining camp. We would roll the 45-gallon drums out of the large cargo door opening and let them drop on the snow, where they remained until they were used. It was cold, and the snow was deep. We each flew a leg –Ron flew the load in, and I flew the plane out empty and helped load and unload. We filled up at Toad River on the Alaska Highway and flew in to the Churchill Mining site on wheel skis.

Ron was the best Otter pilot I ever met and handled the Otter like a Super Cub. He wore thick glasses and was hard of hearing. One of his favorite things to do with a passenger he didn't know who was sitting in the co-pilot's seat was to pretend to lose his glasses and grope around with his hands looking for them, unable to see.

A near whiteout caught us at the end of the job on our way home. I had the maps out navigating. Ron was flying just above the blowing snow. At times we could see only a few hundred feet ahead. We arrived in Smithers after winding for hours through some narrow valleys.

The snow was slow leaving, but spring finally arrived. The ice was gone from the Bulkley River by May. The moose that we saw behind our log cabin during winter were gone now to the higher country. My restless spirit, dormant during the winter, now stirred, and I longed to be flying in the Yukon Territory once again.

On May 18, 1970 I packed a flight jacket, log books and some clothes in my 1967 Volkswagen bug. Smithers fell behind as I drove east toward Prince George, then north for Dawson Creek and the beginning of the Alaska Highway and another season in the Yukon.

Jack O'Conner on the left, Larry Whitesitt and a hunter. I flew Jack into Frank Cook's camp on Colt Lake and be shot a Stone Sheep. Jack was the outdoor editor for Outdoor Life magazine and I eagerly read his hunting stories as I was growing up.

A Beaver Float Plane that Frank Cook leased with a pilot. After taking off of Colt Lake, BC (a small lake) he made a steep climbing turn and stalled it. He survived but was badly injured.

Larry Whitesitt standing on the float of Beaver CF-JBP that he flew for B.C. Yukon Air Service at Watson Lake, Yukon in 1969 and 1970. The dock was at their headquarters on Watson Lake.

Left, Frank Cook, his wife Hattie, son Terry Cook and Larry Whitesitt. This is Moodie Lake where Frank had his main hunting camp in 1969 where I met him. Later he moved his main camp to Scoop Lake!

A DC-3 at Frank Cook's airstrip at Scoop Lake, his main hunting camp in
Northern British Columbia.

Chapter 3

YUKON CO-PILOT

S cott, my cheerful 10-year-old son and wife Kathy are going on a flight with me in our company's single engine de Havilland Otter float plane to Blue Sheep Lake. The lake is about 70 miles south in a wilderness area of northern British Columbia.

Kathy and Scott left our log cabin home in the peaceful Bulkley River Valley a few miles east of Smithers, British Columbia when Scott's school let out for the summer and joined me at the small town of Watson Lake in the Yukon. It's their first time in the Yukon and my second flying season for B.C. Yukon Air Service at Watson Lake. It was June 19, 1970 as we began loading freight into the Otter off our dock on Watson Lake, which is about a mile south of the airport.

It's our first flight together in an Otter, as I usually fly a de Havilland Beaver float plane, but the Otter hauls twice the payload of a Beaver, and it is especially useful for large freight that won't fit inside a Beaver.

I'm a flight instructor and let Scott fly the floatplanes once we were airborne and not carrying passengers. He is a safe, cautious pilot and takes flying seriously. Bush pilots in Watson Lake fly long hours seven days a week during our busy summer and fall season, so when Scott takes the controls, it gives me a welcome break to stretch my legs, relax and watch the wilderness slip beneath our wings.

After loading the Otter, I started the 600-horsepower Pratt & Whitney radial engine, taxied out into the lake and went through my pre-flight check list, CIGFTPR – controls, instruments, gas, flaps, trim, prop, run-up – turned into the wind, lifted the water rudder, advanced the throttle and flew off the lake into the wilderness.

It was an interesting flight with the last couple miles through a winding narrow canyon. The lake wasn't visible until the last minute or so before landing. Blue Sheep Lake is very small, which keeps you on your toes and makes for a challenging approach and landing. Throttle back, landing flaps and we touch down on the east side close to shore. By the time we were off the step we were on the other end of the lake. Some men from the mining exploration camp met me at the shore, and we soon unloaded an assortment of mail, groceries and mining supplies. Coming out light, having only some core samples and mail, the Otter was on the step and in the air before half the lake was used up. One day one of these men swallowed battery acid, thinking it was water, and his throat started to swell closed. I flew in and brought him to Watson Lake, where he was treated successfully.

The flight back to Watson Lake went smoothly. This mining exploration company had set up their summer camp beside the lake. They called us on the radio when they needed supplies. They had a helicopter, so we flew fuel in for the chopper. The Otter can haul six 45-gallon drums of fuel; the Beaver usually hauls three 45-gallon drums, but I have hauled four drums on short hauls when I am light on fuel. Some of the mining companies hired helicopter pilots that flew in the Vietnam War, and they are very good, dropping off geologists on the ledges and on top of mountain peaks.

Blue Sheep Lake is in a specially designated wilderness area of northeast British Columbia called the Northern Rocky Mountain Wilderness Area. The borders are from the Peace River in the south to the Yukon border in the north and from the Rocky Mountains in the east to the Cassiar Mountains in the west.

Bruce McClellan, a noted grizzly bear biologist said, "This area has the largest diversification of big game animals in the world outside of Africa; it's the Serengeti of North America, and it's a national treasure." Flying over this area is like looking at a game farm, as I watched moose, mountain caribou, mountain goats, stone sheep and grizzly bears in large numbers.

Blue Sheep Lake is one of George Dalziel's big game hunting camps that he guides from. In British Columbia where Dalziel guides, he is given a designated area to hunt. In Alaska a guide can hunt any place. Resident hunters can hunt any place.

Kathy expedites for Dal and does an excellent job at picking up his hunters at the airport and supplies for his camps. She brings them to our base, and we fly them out to his hunting camps. Kathy, Scott and I visit Dal and his wife June at their log home in Watson Lake, which is across from the log Watson Lake Hotel.

Dal is an old time original "bush pilot" who has been flying in the north since the 1930s. He started B.C. Yukon Air Service and purchased some of the first de Havilland Beavers that were first produced in the late 1940s. He is a legend of the north. The lakes in the north have native lake trout, but some have rainbow trout. I have been told Dal has stocked some of the lakes with rainbow trout from his floatplane. Dal flies a Super Cub on floats.

Scott was now ten years old and, as always, enjoyed himself wherever he was. Scott and I were very close, and he made a good co-pilot. He also pumped the floats and helped clean my airplane.

Norm Simmons, a game biologist for the Canadian government, called our base from Norman Wells, Northwest Territories, and requested the Beaver for a few days. On July 9, 1970 I prepared to depart for Norm's camp on the Keel River. Kathy and Scott were going with me on this flight. It was new country for all of us and the furthest north we had been yet, not far from the Arctic Circle. The Keel River camp was located about 80 miles southwest of Norman Wells and 290 miles northeast of Watson Lake. It would take about two and one-half flying hours to reach there.

We followed the Hyland River almost to the Northwest Territories, crossed the South Nahanni River, and followed the Brokenskull River to the headwaters of the Natla River. Following the Natla we soon flew over Rex Logan's hunting camp, just below where the Natla enters the Keel River. From here it was about a hundred miles downstream to Norm Simmons' camp, which was a few miles above Nainli Creek.

I could see a small dock on the north bank of the keel. The cabin was located on a bench that ran parallel to the river. The river appeared very swift, white water tumbled the surface, and some mean-looking rapids and jagged rocks were visible about 400 feet downstream from the dock. It was going to be a "stay on your toes every second" landing and docking, but I enjoyed the challenge and looked the river over carefully as I circled and planned my approach. The river told a story that I read very carefully, looking for the deeper, safer channels before making my landing. It was a wild river, and I treated it with the respect it deserved.

The river was in a mountainous valley, and the only reason Norm Simmons didn't fly with a flying service company out of Norman Wells was that they didn't like mountain flying and landing on swift rivers. Pilots like that were what I called "flat land pilots," flying the level country east of the rugged Mackenzie Mountains.

My decision was made, and we made an approach, slowing down to about 65 miles per hour indicated on final landing. I touched down and came off the step just before the dock. I needed lots of power to hold my own against the current as I started to work my way carefully toward the dock. Nudging up to the dock, I left the power on until I was securely tied, not daring to shut down until then. Usually I landed into the current where you have better control. You can go forward, or back up while heading for the shore with the engine running.

Norm updated me on his study. Perry Lynton had been flying a Helio Courier for him, using it to spray the sheep with red dye so they could keep track of their habits. He had kept his plane on a makeshift strip on the bench by the cabin, but a flood washed the plane away, completely destroying it. Norm and his assistants climbed up in the attic of the cabin, as the main floor was underwater, and waited out the flood. Perry's plane was uninsured, and he suffered considerable loss, as the Helio was a very expensive plane. Norm's a friendly, straightforward kind of man who was doing a study of Dall sheep here in the Mackenzie Mountains. They used a cage trap to catch the sheep and then measured and checked them over. After putting tags on them, they turned them loose!

We stayed a couple of days. I flew Norm to Norman Wells, where he picked up supplies and took care of some business, and then we flew back to camp. Norman Wells had an oil refinery. During World War II a pipeline was laid to the south, and for a while oil was pumped. Old pumping stations can still be seen along the old Canal Road. I also flew the Beaver to Fort Good Hope, an Indian Village on the Mackenzie River near the Arctic Circle.

Norm had a very large, magnificent malamute dog that must have weighed 150 pounds or more. The malamute, a close descendant of the wolf, doesn't bark much, but he howls like a wolf. Norm's was a good-natured, quiet dog that had a presence and knew he was the boss of his domain. Scott talked to an old Indian man who worked for Norm and first came to the Keel in a skin canoe when he was a child. He and his wife lived in a cabin nearby, and their sled dogs would sometimes start howling. The old Indian woman would go outside and tap on a stump with a stick, and they instantly quieted down. After several side trips for Norm, Kathy, Scott and I departed for Watson Lake and arrived there after a smooth, uneventful flight.

Jack Hodge, who had been the manager of Omineca Air Service and invited me to go for a check ride in the Cub, which led to my first job, was here in Watson Lake. I was glad to see Jack, as he was an interesting, experienced pilot (as well as an engineer) and had always treated me well.

Jack was flying an Aero Star, a fast, light twin-engine airplane that was used as a bird dog for the World War II A-26 twin-engine bombers converted to water bombers that were working a fire near here. Jack made a run over the fire first and then radioed the 26s of any problems before they began their runs. The A-26 required only one pilot, and it looked like an exciting flying job.

The lead pilot told me I should consider getting into this type of work, as I was the kind of pilot, with my bush flying experience and hours flown, that they were looking for. He seemed to me to be a bit of a hot dogger, as he always tried to pin the plane on the very end of the runway when he landed, sometimes landing short and sending up a huge dust cloud as he hit the dirt and grass.

This lead pilot was working a fire after leaving Watson Lake. He would fly above a ridge and follow down a canyon, dropping his load as he descended. He decided to fly up the draw with a full load and got behind the power curve, stalled out and killed himself within two weeks of our conversation.

The other pilot, a "recently ex-Canadian Air Force" type, was flying up the Frazer River in an A-26 bomber about two weeks after he left Watson Lake, got in some bad weather and tried to climb through it. He almost made it but hit the top of a peak and was killed. The chief pilot for the same company was also killed in a DC-6, along with two crewmembers while dropping water on a fire. He evidently stalled in a turn, again within about two weeks of my conversation with the A-26 pilot who encouraged me to get into this type of flying.

On a nice summer day in 1968 on Maclure Lake, Sheldon Luck, a famous early-day bush pilot then in his sixties, flew in as the pilot of a converted PBY called a Cansol. Sheldon was one of the finest and most experienced pilots in this type of work; he was a living legend, well known and respected in the aviation world. He was the father of Grant Luck, who was the base manager after jack Hodge left. Bill Harrison and his partner Alec Davidson bought the PBY flying boats from a company called Flying Firemen to use as water bombers to drop water and chemicals on fires.

In the fall of 1968 Bill Harrison asked if I would be interested in going to Tasmania, an island off Australia, as a copilot on one of the Cansols. I gave a quick affirmative, and he continued, "We may have a contract for this winter down there." It didn't materialize.

The following summer one of these Cansols crashed while working a fire, and both crewmembers were killed. Alec and his copilot were flying a Super Cansol, which had larger engines and hauled about 1200 gallons of water. The other Cansols hauled 800 gallons. A wing tore off while they were dropping water on a fire on Vancouver Island, and they were both killed. Sheldon Luck was flying the other plane. A season or two later I heard another one of the Cansols and crew were lost on a fire – a very risky business. Visibility was poor, as they had to get so low to make an effective drop. The longevity of a pilot in this line of work is short.

The rustic-looking B.C. Yukon Air Service seaplane office was built out of panobode-type logs. We had a long dock and a storage shed. At the airport by the main terminal was a large World War II hangar that B.C. Yukon owned, where major work was done on the airplanes. Frontier Helicopters, which was owned by Sid Baird, Bill Harrison and others, also used this hangar for helicopter maintenance.

A radio operator and dispatcher monitored the single sideband radio, kept in touch with the pilots as they flew to their various destinations, and gave advice on weather. If there was a problem with your airplane or you got into bad weather, it was great to know someone was at the base to take our call and help out.

Mark Goostry, a warm, likeable eighteen-year-old new pilot with a sunny disposition and quick smile, was flying the Super Cub for B.C. Yukon. One warm summer day he crashed into a mountainside by Wolverine Lake in northern B.C. I was at the base when I was told about the accident, which rolled the Super Cut into a mass of fabric and metal while Mark walked away without injury. My comment was, "Good, now we're rid of that poor performing Super Cub." It was a dog, and the margin of safety was little, as the cruising speed wasn't much higher than the stall speed. I also commented, "Now, maybe we'll get a good performing Super Cub." Mark later in his flying career was flying a twin-engine Otter on floats between Vancouver and Victoria, British Columbia when he was killed. The flaps were down as he made the approach to land. All of a sudden, the connecting rod to one of the flaps broke due to corrosion (mechanical failure), causing the airplane to roll and crash into the ocean. Mark and nine of the eleven Japanese passengers were killed – the co-pilot survived. Mark loved to fly and was doing what he enjoyed when the end came.

Dennis Ball was flying the de Havilland Otter most of the time. Dennis was killed a couple years later in the Otter. He was flying for a mining company in the rugged Mackenzie Mountains in bad weather and went up a blind canyon and crashed along with one passenger who was killed. Most of the pilots who were killed when I flew were because of bad weather.

Occasionally I made a trip with the Otter, but I preferred the Beaver, although it was interesting to fly different types from time to time. Max Sanderson, an old-time Beaver pilot and then helicopter pilot for Cannex Mining Company gave his definition for a good Otter pilot – someone who wore a size four hat, was four feet tall and about as wide. The ceiling in the Otter is about five feet tall, so you have to bend over while loading the plane, and it's just a lot of hard work hauling freight. In the Beaver you had a lot of passengers and not so much freight.

Grant Luck and Sid Baird were in charge of operations, and Grant helped out with the flying. We all got along well. Flights often began at 0400, and sometimes we flew as late as 2200. We were paid a good base salary and five to ten cents a mile, depending on the type of airplane flown. The season was short, so we tried to get in as many miles as possible.

One hot summer day Grant told the engineer to put the water tanks on the Beaver. A forest fire had broken out by the lake and was threatening to burn up the town of Watson Lake a few miles south. A 90-gallon dump tank was mounted on each float. There was a tube running from the tank down to the water that filled the tanks in a matter of seconds while the plane was on the step. (The step, which is located in the middle of the float and looks – appropriately enough – like a step, is where the airplane rides when it planes at high speeds.)

After the installation, a senior pilot decided to fly the first few drops, and we taxied for takeoff. Fortunately, the engine quit before we took off, as the fuel selector valve was inadvertently on an empty tank. He selected the full tank, started the engine, and we were soon on the step and filling up the tanks, then on our way to the fire.

Diving down on the fire and pulling the release cable, we zoomed up as the heavy weight of the water instantly left the tanks. It was rather exciting, acting like a bomber. After a couple of drops, the senior pilot got off at the dock, and I finished the day dropping water on the fire. It was a nice change, and it made me imagine I was in a war and dropping bombs. A helicopter with a long cable and bucket was also being used.

The fire was put out, and the town was saved from becoming a burnt spot on the map.

This was a bad year for fires. We flew forestry personnel and equipment to areas without roads, as they tried to control the many fires burning through the vast area. The Cub was used to fly a forestry patrol route, looking for telltale smoke. On floats the Cub hardly seemed to move, and four or five hours in its hard seat was about all you could take.

I had an interesting fun flight with Dave, the Forest Ranger at Lower Post, British Columbia, which is about 15 miles south of Watson Lake, just inside the British Columbia border. Lower Post is an Indian village. Dave chartered B.C. Yukon's Cessna 185. I flew to Lower Post, landed on the Liard River, picked up Dave and two other forestry employees and departed for Denetiah Lake. We did some fishing on a stream at the west end of the lake, which flows into Denetiah from a small lake about a half mile to the southwest. This was the best fishing I had ever experienced, and I have the picture of our catch, which was also used in Frank Cooke's brochure on fishing.

We caught about 74 rainbow trout in a couple hours and kept 32 that weighed between two and nine pounds. The ice had recently gone out and the fish were active and struck hard. I believe these rainbow trout were planted by the old bush pilot, George Dalziel from his floatplane. We fished until we had our fill, then we flew back to Lower Post and I dropped them off on the banks of the Liard River. I returned to B.C. Yukon's float base with my fabulous fish story, documented with a picture from the trusty Argus C-3 35mm camera that I purchased years ago from a destitute sailor on my ship in the South Pacific. In fact, all but a few of the pictures I took while flying in the North were taken with this solid camera.

In August I flew the Beaver into Fort Simpson, which is located at the junction of the Liard and Mackenzie Rivers in the Northwest Territories. There was a fire nearby, and I flew fuel into it for the aircraft and helicopter that were fighting the fire. I flew over eight hours that day and was fairly tired after many hours of loading 45-gallon drums of aviation gas in and out of the Beaver. The day went quickly and after a good meal at a local hotel, I got a room there and was soon asleep. Morning came quickly, and I started another day of hauling fuel to the fire. After another rather long day I returned to Watson Lake. Kathy and Scott returned to our log home, and Scott went back to school. Kathy is a wonderful mother to Scott, and they are very close. Kathy returned to her job with Laurence Perry, an attorney, at Smithers BC.

The long summer days passed quickly, as I worked seven days a week with many long hours. Eight hours of flying time usually required a good 16-hour day because of loading, unloading and waiting time. On September 23, 1970 I flew the Cessna into Wolverine and Dease Lake and back to Watson Lake on the last flight of the season for B.C. Yukon Air Service at Watson Lake. My total time now was 2620 hours.

In October I returned once again to Galvin's Flight Service at Boeing Field in Seattle and began training for my Airline Transport Pilot license (ATP) rating. After putting in four days in a Cherokee 140, I began flying a Piper Aztec PA-23, which was a twin-engine executive-type airplane that I used to train for the ATP rating. It was more difficult to fly – much faster – and it kept me on my toes. On every flight it seemed my instructor pulled an engine while I was under the hood or in actual instrument conditions. In addition to flying with instruments, I also had to contend with a lost engine, and it kept me busy just trying to stay up with the airplane and stay on course.

The written test for the Airline Transport Pilot rating was difficult, and I had to learn nine formulas by heart, just to work out the math and engineering problems. Math was never a strong point of mine. After much study and restudy I finally passed the written. On December 7, 1970 my logbook says, "ATP passed – Frank Benedict." Frank was the designated inspector for the FAA and took me on the flight check ride, which is similar to an instrument check ride only you have to be much more precise in flight maneuvers and your ability to hold the correct altitude and heading. Red-letter day – my pilot license now reads Airline Transport Pilot.

Single engine Otter, like the one Scott and Kathy flew with me up to Blue Sheep Lake owned by Watson Lake Flying Services at their dock.

George (Dal) Dalziel, an early day bush pilot and outfitter on the left, Kathy, Larry, and Dal's wife June Dalziel, Marco Polo sheep in the background in Dal's home, Watson Lake, summer of 1970.

Left: Scott & Kathy Whitesitt next to Prime Minister Trudeau, Lynn Thibaudeau, whose husband, Jim, was killed in the Beech 18 in 1975, airplane mechanics wife, and Mrs. Ball with her arm around her son. Her husband, Dennis Ball, was killed in B.C. Yukon, single engine Otter in the Northwest Territories in bad weather, and my uncle Floyd. The Prime Minister was on a campaign trip for reelection in 1970.

Larry Whitesitt on the right, Dave the Forest Ranger at Lower Post in the middle and a forestry worker. We caught about 70 rainbow trout at Denatiah Lake, B.C. and kept 32 between 2 and 9 pounds.

I flew Rex Handcock, a hunter from the United States
out of Stevens Lake, B.C. with this grizzly bear that he
shot with a bow and it was a world record.

Left is Bill Love my neighbor and a hunting guide. Middle is Fred Bear,
maker of the Bear Bow. And the one on the right is my boyhood hero Fess
Parker who played Davy Crocket in the movies. He was my boyhood hero
in the 50's. Fess Parker shot a grizzly bear close to where Larry flew out the
world record grizzly bear shot with a bow by Rex Hancock near Stevens
Lake, BC.

Chapter 4

THE RED BEAVER

Flying the Red Beaver CF-IBP for the first time on May 31, 1971 was my official check ride for my new employer, Watson Lake Flying Service. Jim Close and Stan Bridcut, his partner, started Watson Lake Flying Service in 1962. They had the oldest flying service in the Yukon that was still in operation with the original owners. They started out with a Piper PA-14 and a Cessna 180.

The flight office was a small building about 50 feet from the lake, consisting of a waiting room, a storeroom, kitchen, a front office, with a back room for the radio and office records. Floatplanes were tied up to a long dock in front of the office. Wally Waulkonan, a big Fin, was our engineer and did most of the maintenance on our planes, including engine changes, normal inspections every 50 hours and daily troubleshooting. Wally was well qualified, having worked many years in Meadow Portage, Manitoba in an engine overhaul shop. He worked for B.C. Yukon Air Service from 1967 to 1970 and has been employed since then by Jim and Stan. Wally and Jim Close, who is also an excellent engineer, worked closely together on airplane maintenance.

Jim Close was about 35 with a twinkle in his eye and an unending repertoire of one-liners. He was a congenial walking encyclopedia of flying history and of the Yukon characters, many of whom he knew personally. He was warm-hearted and often too easy in extending credit to people who were down on their luck. Trappers, outfitters and others who needed to fly into the bush but were without funds found a sympathetic ear and an airplane to drop them off at their various camps or homes.

Jim Close was the front man, the visible one most people first saw or talked to when booking a flight or arriving at the float dock. He was the organizer and kept the company running. He operated the radio and kept in touch with people in the bush. When Jim and Stan first started Watson Lake Flying Service in 1962, Jim was doing some of the flying and was written up in a local paper for a rescue operation he performed. His expertise as the engineer for the company eventually consumed most of his time, and he gave up being an active pilot, however, he still flew enough to check out the airplanes he worked on.

Stan Bridcut, Jim's partner, was in his forties, lean and wiry, with a quick grin and quiet demeanor. His flying experience covered a long span, and he had a wealth of knowledge about bush flying that took some prodding to uncover. He didn't talk much about himself. Jim Thibaudeau, whom I first met when we both flew for B.C. Yukon Air Service, flew for Watson Lake Flying Service while I was there.

Wally Waulkonan and his wife Marge and children live near the seaplane base and have a comfortable home on the water, close to Jim Thibaudeau's lake place north of the base. Wally is good natured and nice to be around, and I was glad to have him working on the Beaver I flew.

Jim flew the Beech 18 on floats most of the time and was a very competent pilot. He had recently married Lynn, and the young couple was well liked by clients and by the local people at Watson Lake.

Bob Mitchell, a young pilot with a few seasons under his belt, flew the Cessna 185 and was also cutting his teeth on the Beaver, which of course he liked. Later Bob went to work for Canadian Pacific Airline, so this was a stepping-stone for him.

John Poiser flew the Super Cub and the Cessna 185. I got to know John well and eventually introduced him to his wife-to-be, a schoolteacher from the Seattle area. John and I lived together for a time at Stan's cabin on the Lake. John was a good pilot and very conscientious, and I liked being around him.

In the many years I flew for Jim and Stan, I never had an engine or structural failure. Once the hydraulic system went out in the Beaver, and I had no flaps when I landed, as they operate hydraulically. It was the only system I can recall that quit working while I was actually flying.

The town of Watson Lake was named after fur trader Frank Watson, who set up a post in the area during the 1890s. Watson Lake was founded with the construction of the airport in 1940. Airplanes that were flown to Russia on the lend-lease program to help in the war effort stopped here for fuel. Many ended up in the bush, due to bad weather and inexperienced pilots, from fighters to bombers. In fact, one valley east of Smith River was called "Million Dollar Valley" because of the planes that crashed there. Three bombers were trying to locate the airport at Smith River in a snowstorm. They followed their leader, and all three landed in Muskeg in the wrong valley – the next valley to the east. I saw the bombers on many occasions when I flew into Dempsey Collison hunting camps in the Scatter River country east of there. They are lined up, one behind the other, in a neat row, the engines long since removed.

When the Alcan Highway was completed in 1942, businesses were established in Watson Lake to cater to the tourists who would eventually use the highway. Today the tourists often stay overnight before continuing on to Whitehorse to the northwest or Fort Nelson to the east, both 250 or more miles distant.

The town is also a center and jumping-off place for prospectors, hunters and fishermen, who often charter flights with Watson Lake Flying Service to fly into remote lakes or airstrips scattered throughout the Yukon, Northwest Territories, or northern British Columbia.

The Yukoners are a casual, laid-back kind of people. If a job doesn't get done today or tomorrow, it can always be done next week or next month. For people used to fast service, this is not the place to come. But if you want to be accepted for yourself, this is the place to be. The Yukoners accept individuals for what they are as persons, not impressed by money or some high position on the outside. Many wealthy men of high position that we flew out to fishing and hunting camps soon learned that lesson.

I once flew the chairman of the board of Standard Oil of New Jersey and several of his underlings to a camp in northern B.C. with the red Beaver. We stayed at this camp for about a week or so. They brought in quite a bit of high-priced booze, and the cook got into the sauce during the night. When we sat down for breakfast the following morning, these oil men were in for an unwelcome surprise that I found quite amusing. The cook was in another world and feeling no pain. In fact, I don't think he could feel; it was surprising he could stand. The pancakes that didn't get flipped on the floor were mostly raw, and these men just weren't used to anything like this. They had to pay for three hours of flying each day, even if they didn't fly, so I mentioned one day that maybe they would like to see some of the country and use up the time they were paying for. This struck them a funny – three hours wasn't much to them, and they weren't concerned about the cost. We flew through the mountains looking for mineral deposits and stopped to do some fishing. They were treated the same as anyone else by the people in the north and by our company.

"ALLIGATORS TO GRIZZLY BEARS"

"LONGEST FLIGHT, FORT MEYERS TO WATSON LAKE"

I began my longest flight as a commercial pilot on June 7, 1971, departing Watson Lake for Fort Meyers, Florida, to pick up a Beaver on floats and fly it back to Watson Lake. A trip from the southeast corner of the United States to the far-off Yukon in the farthest northwest part of Canada excited me with the anticipation of new adventures and new country – and getting well paid for what was almost a pleasure flight.

I flew the commercial airlines to Toronto and from there to Florida. After arriving in Fort Meyers, I spent three days from June 8 to June 11 working with an airplane mechanic to help get the airplane ready for the flight north.

On June 11, I climbed into the white de Havilland Beaver, cranked it up and began taxiing toward the center of the river. After a satisfactory run-up, I applied full power and came close to an alligator swimming in the river. I had previously filled two 45-gallon drums of aviation fuel to use as a reserve, which I tied securely behind the pilot's seat. There are few seaplane bases in the South, and the extra fuel came in handy on numerous occasions during this long flight. The blue-green ocean of the Gulf of Mexico was under my left wing as I followed the Florida coast. This magnificent sky-blue day, new scenery and the freedom of at last starting my journey home made my spirits soar!

The friendly skies began turning dark and ominous after about an hour, and I turned away from the coast in order to skirt the darkest thunderstorm. My fuel was getting low, and I wasn't certain where I was, because I couldn't get aviation maps of this area.

Below I saw a narrow canal winding by a few cabins, and I noticed some signs of life. After a normal approach and landing, I tied up to the bank and walked to the nearest cabin. A couple of women looked at me curiously; they hadn't heard me land. I explained my mission and asked for directions to New Orleans, as that was the day's destination. They pointed toward New Orleans and gave me an idea of the distance.

My fuel was low, so I ran a hose with a wobble pump attached from the drums to the belly tanks and began transferring fuel. It took a fair amount of time to fill the tanks, but at last they were topped.

The temperature and humidity were high as I began my takeoff run on the canal. At the last possible moment, just before the canal made a ninety-degree turn to the left, I managed to stagger into the air. When I arrived in New Orleans several hours later, I noticed weeds and twigs wound around the water rudders, from skimming along the bushes just above the ground after takeoff with the floats. The engine was on the weak side, and I think it had a lot more hours on it than the engine logbook showed. In other words, it was about clapped out. Later when the company replaced the engine with a rebuilt one, I understand it performed well.

I disliked, maybe hated, this Beaver, and so did the company pilots. Luckily for me, it was given to a fairly new pilot, Bob Mitchell, who later flew for Canadian Pacific Airline. This was his first Beaver, and after flying the Cessna 185, he thought it was a marvelous machine. I was sure glad to get IBP back.

I stayed overnight in New Orleans and spent most of the evening walking Bourbon Street in the French Quarter. I listened to a terrific jazz band, four black men in their sixties and seventies playing horns – they were terrific. In the morning I worked on the airplane, installing a new battery.

I departed from New Orleans for Memphis, Tennessee on June 12. I landed on a small lake to refuel, where I came close to a bad mishap, because some wire was strung across the lake and wasn't marked. I just touched down as the wire passed overhead, appearing to be too low to miss, but fortunately I did. After transferring fuel, I departed.

I landed on the Mississippi River a few miles north of Memphis and tied up to an island. I got a ride to the boat landing from a yacht owner, as there were a number of yachts pulled up and anchored along the island where a group of wealthy people were on a weekend outing. I was fortunate to find a man driving up, as it was late and deserted at the landing. He asked me what I was doing. I explained that I had just landed on the river with the Beaver and needed a lift into town. He told me to take his car, because he was going to stay overnight on his boathouse, but to make sure and bring it back by noon the next day. Southern hospitality at its finest, I thought, as I left for Memphis, which was about seven miles away.

The next day I flew from Memphis to St. Louis and overnighted there, then went to Madison Wisconsin, where I stayed overnight at a motel owned by an interesting inventor. One of his inventions was a large car with truck tires that you walked into from the rear, standing up straight. It had an oil furnace for heat. While at Madison, I had some papers signed by the former owner of the Beaver, releasing the airplane.

An interesting story was told to me by the airplane mechanic in Fort Meyers who had helped me get the airplane ready for my departure. The Beaver had been in a South American country which had a revolution, making the legal removal of the plane impossible. The owner persuaded a U.S. pilot to fly it out of the country, which he succeeded in doing, after obtaining the necessary fuel from various places. Well, he flew it out of the country and into the United States, illegally and at great risk, but he didn't obtain the remuneration he had been promised.

From Madison I flew to St. Paul, Minnesota, a three-hour flight. I arrived in good form and spent the night with Mike, the owner of the Beaver, who was leasing it to our company. A few stories were told about the far north before we parted company that night.

The next day I departed for Estavan, Saskatchewan. On the way, I stopped in North Dakota and filled up the belly tanks from the two 45-gallon drums on board. I landed and cleared customs in Estavan, then flew almost to Edmonton. I stopped on a small lake when it got too dark to fly and slept at a nearby motel. All I remember of that stay is waking up and getting a ride to the plane the following morning.

When I arrived at Edmonton, I ended up staying for ten days, because a lot of work needed to be done in order to get the Beaver licenses with a Certificate of Airworthiness.

On June 27, 1971 I cranked up the white Beaver CF-WMH and departed Edmonton for Dawson Creek, a three-hour flight. Battery trouble forced me to stay overnight at Dawson. Then I headed up the Rocky Mountain Trench on a course to Watson Lake. As I had on the whole trip, I carried extra fuel in two drums. I had to make one stop on a lake in the Rocky Mountain Trench to transfer fuel to my front and middle tanks. The trip from Dawson Creek to Watson Lake totaled four flying hours, plus the short stop to transfer fuel.

Such an extended trip across North America was quite an event to begin my flying with this new company. It was 17 days from departure at Fort Meyers, where an alligator was swimming in the river at takeoff, to arrival in the far north Yukon Territory, where the grizzly bear is king! This was also the beginning of a series of new adventures that would forever be special highlights in my aviation career.

Toward the end of June I flew some people into Seaplane Lake, which is by the Flat River in the Northwest Territories. I flew into this lake on many occasions over the years. We were flying my favorite airplane, the red Beaver CF-IBP. My passengers were going to raft down the Flat River to the South Nahanni River. I also flew the white

Beaver CF-WMH into Burnt Rose Lake, 80 miles south, near the Turnagain River where the outfitter Johnny Drift had a hunting camp.

Later that day I flew into Don Taylor's place on Stewart Lake, 40 miles north in the Yukon Territory. He had constructed a nice lodge and some cabins. Don, a local politician, represented Watson Lake and the surrounding area. He spent much of his time in Whitehorse during sessions, pushing the needs of the people in his district. He was developing a sport fishing business and planned to retire here one day. The fishing is good, with red trout colored like salmon from the freshwater shrimp they eat. Don was always friendly, and I enjoyed flying for him. He had strong feelings about the government of the Yukon, of course, and worked hard for his district.

July 6th I flew into Windy Point, where a big game outfitters' hunting camp was located beside the Turnagain River. The Turnagain is, as the name implies, a river with many turns. It is shallow and a bit tricky at Windy Point. Landing upstream and working against the current to shore isn't too bad; however, because it is so shallow and has large boulders, it is imperative to land in the deepest channel. Take-off is a bit tricky on this windy, narrow river. If the wind is blowing downstream, the airplane wants to stay weathercocked into the wind and current, and you can lose a lot of distance trying to turn downwind for takeoff if, as is the case on portions of this river because of obstructions upstream, you have to take off downstream.

Earl Boose's camp on the Turnagain near Sandpile Creek, which I often flew into, required a downstream takeoff in an easterly direction. The wind is usually from the west there, so I normally had a tailwind, and it could get tricky turning and then getting airborne with a sharp bend fairly close downstream. It was then a matter of full power with a tailwind and a fast current, with the pilot white-knuckling the controls as you went around the first bend on the step or maybe flying and trying to get altitude so you could climb above the trees along the bank before another sharp bend gave you another gray hair or two, or worse.

A green eighteen-year-old pilot put our Super Cub in near Windy Point. It hit so hard that the wings actually broke off the fuselage and dropped the wingtips into the water, and the floats broke loose from the struts and bent upward. Neither the pilot nor the passenger was injured, but the pilot ended up gassing planes for the remainder of his time with Watson Lake Flying Service. A picture of his mishap is in an album there – it looks like a bird shot out of the sky.

Over the next several days I flew to Twin, Nome, Allen, Davis and John I Lakes. I also flew the Cessna 185 CF-YIG into Tobally Lakes, which are 80 miles east of our base and in the Yukon Territories. Larry Schnig had a fishing camp there where you could catch huge lake trout, large pike and Arctic grayling.

One beautiful summer day I flew to Virginia Falls, a favorite place of mine, with some people who wanted to take pictures. Virginia Falls, which is twice as high as Niagara Falls, is located about 150 miles northeast of Watson Lake in the Northwest Territories. We flew in the red Beaver floatplane.

This flight took about an hour and twenty minutes. We flew at about 7,000 feet, passing over the Hyland and Coal Rivers and Skinboat Lakes, north of McMillan Lake, and across the flat about 16 miles south of the falls. As we circled the falls, the passengers got some good pictures. We began our letdown and on final flew over the falls and landed just above the rapids, about 2,000 feet above the falls. Taxiing into shore, I jumped out and securely tied the plane down. If it went over the falls, we would have a long walk home.

There was a large boat decaying near the beach. The boat had been hauled up piece by piece from below the falls and reassembled to be used on the water upstream – quite a feat getting it up board by board on a man's back. Albert Faille, the noted Nahanni explorer, was that man.

After a few hours of picture taking, walking to the falls, and getting some close-ups, we climbed aboard. The reliable radial engine started after a couple of revolutions of the prop. Soon we were on the step, speeding upstream away from the falls. Slight back pressure and the reliable Beaver was in its element. We continued upstream over the river to gain a safe altitude before heading southwest back to Watson Lake.

My passengers were impressed and well satisfied with this magnificent set of falls.

The federal government eventually made this area and the land for many miles downstream past Deadman's Valley, into Nahanni National Park. It was a worthwhile effort to set this magnificent wilderness aside for future generations. This park is much larger than Yellowstone Park in the United States.

I had a trip to Rabbit Kettle Hot Springs, just south of the South Nahanni River. Summer was passing swiftly – it was already August 3rd. Soon the trees would begin turning gold in the high country. The publisher of an Anchorage newspaper, his wife and a friend stood on the dock, watching as I tied their canoe to the floats. The canoe sat on top of the float, the bottom facing outward. I used two ropes at each end of the canoe, each tied around the bottom of the float struts, wrapped around the canoe, looped around the top of the strut and then back through the middle to a loop in the rope and cinched until they were tight as a bowstring. The canoe was then ready to fly safely.

I was always very careful with external loads and never had one get away, but I heard stories of some pilots who did. Once I flew an 18-foot boat that weighed about 400 pounds. I loaded it onto the Beaver from a lake by myself, with much grunting and some mumbling, because it was not only heavy but awkward to handle as well. Antlers were by far the hardest things to fly with, as they disturbed the air flow so that the Beaver shuddered and didn't like to fly. Such a load slowed the plane down about 40 miles per hour to an indicated 80 miles per hour once when I had seven caribou racks tied on the outside.

A canoe or boat slowed me down about 10 miles an hour, making it a little wing heavy and causing the airplane to yaw slightly, but it flew relatively well. Sometimes I flew sheets of plywood and lumber in the same manner without any problem. I flew a radial engine, tied to the floats, into a lake in northern B.C. for our Beech 18, when Jim Thibaudeau lost an engine and made an emergency landing there. The company has a picture of it in their album.

When the canoe was securely tied down to my satisfaction, we climbed aboard and pushed out to deeper waters. I engaged the starter and the engine coughed, sputtered and roared to life, ready for another trip. The red Beaver looked a little strange with this object hanging out on the port side but took it in stride. The takeoff run was longer with the external load, but we were soon in the air and climbing on a northerly heading to the fabled South Nahanni River.

The flight was pleasant, as the weather was sunny with excellent visibility. We followed the Coal River to its source and then flew over the Flat River about 30 miles south of our destination. We landed near the hot springs, untied the canoe and pulled it up to shore, then unloaded the supplies.

Our party planned to head downstream to Virginia Falls, portage along a steep trail on the south side to the bottom of the falls and continue downriver. The distance from the hot springs to Virginia Falls is about 52 air miles, but it's much farther by canoe, as the river winds and loops.

Deadman's Valley is down the river another 50 air miles. After going through the Grand Canyon of the Nahanni on the other side of the valley, they would reach Kraus's Cabin and Hot Springs, where they would probably have a long, leisurely soak. They would finish the run at Nahanni Butte, about 52 air miles east. This is where the South Nahanni enters the Liard River, and there is an Indian village and a school there. They would use a two-way radio at the school to contact us at Watson Lake when they were ready for me to pick them up.

After wishing them well, I taxied out. The empty Beaver seemed to leap into the air after a very short run, and I began a climbing left turn to the southwest toward Watson Lake, flying directly over the mountains. The flight back took about 1:15. It was pleasant – just me and my favorite airplane on another journey over the fabled Yukon and Northwest Territories. Soon we would be back at our base, preparing for a new adventure. What a pleasant way to live my life: doing what I enjoyed most, and getting paid to do it. I was a fortunate man, and I knew it.

Two days after my trip into Rabbit Kettle Hot Springs, a much longer trip into the Northwest Territories began. The Northwest

Territories Forest Service booked IBP to fly from Watson Lake to Fort Simpson, pick up a fire fighter crew and fly them to Yellowknife. There were some forest fires out of control, and fire fighters were needed right away.

The trip to Fort Simpson is 280 miles, and it's another 270 to Yellowknife, about 550 air miles total. Getting paid mileage plus a base salary made this a very profitable trip. I was also getting to see new country, as it was my first trip to Yellowknife, the capital of the Northwest Territories.

The red Beaver climbed quickly to 8,000 feet, and I headed on a northeasterly course to Fort Simpson, which was located at the junction of the Liard and Mackenzie Rivers, on the southwest side. Fort Simpson was a small town. Several newer buildings were visible as I circled over town and checked the Mackenzie River for driftwood before my final approach. Landing to the east, against the current, I found a fair current running. After shutting off the engine I had to jump out of the Beaver on the passenger side and tie down quickly before we were swept downstream.

I met the forest ranger, and we loaded the Beaver with four men and their gear. I taxied out into the river, checked the controls and instruments, raised the water rudders and applied full power. Because we were near sea level, where the air is denser IBP quickly got on the step; slight back pressure and we broke free of the mighty Mackenzie River and headed almost due east for Yellowknife.

The weather was overcast, but the ceiling was a couple of thousand feet, so we were fat and happy. I was amazed at the countless lakes and swamps under my wings. The relatively flat country that begins east of the Mackenzie River stretched as far as my eyes could see.

Great Slave Lake is over 250 miles long, the longest lake I had ever seen. Yellowknife is on the north side. To see a small city so far north, surrounded by wilderness, was unusual, and it seemed out of place. After unloading the men and gear, I walked through this northern city. It was much like other Canadian cities farther south. Bank buildings, Hudson Bay store, post office, Royal Canadian Mounted Police headquarters and restaurants lined the paved streets. Walking back to the plan after a quick tour, I fueled up and was soon in the air heading west, back to Fort Simpson.

The weather was deteriorating rapidly as I set a compass course. Knowing that I would come over the Mackenzie River, my big concern was that when I did I would make the right decision, turning in the direction of Fort Simpson, unless of course I came out over the town.

The ceiling continued to drop, and I was soon about 150 feet above the trees. Fortunately it was flat country, and I could see under the clouds, but the ceiling had dropped so much since flying over earlier in the day that I was getting concerned, especially since this was my first trip to this area, and I didn't know the country.

Finally the wide Mackenzie, about one mile across at this point, came into sight, and I turned right, downstream, hoping it was the right direction to Fort Simpson. We flew visual flight rules (VFR), as our airplanes were not equipped for instrument flying. Jim Thibaudeau and I were the only pilots in Watson Lake who were instrument rated. Normally I was able to pick out lakes, mountains and rivers that showed up on my map as I navigated to a new area. It was important to get an accurate fix on my location, but the country was flat and the lakes endless, so all the lakes looked alike as I flew low over them. Flying over the Mackenzie River was an improvement – at least I could land, and if my calculations and a little luck were on my side, Fort Simpson should be showing up soon.

Sure enough, it was my lucky day. Ahead I could just make out some buildings that soon became Fort Simpson. What a relief to find my port in a storm. A quick circle over the landing area, and I turned final, landing flaps, quick pre-landing check. Approaching at 80 mph, I soon leveled out and raised the nose to the landing attitude. The floats touched the water, and we settled in like a well-fed duck.

Having been here earlier in the day, I was familiar with the current and easily maneuvered to the dock. After I fueled up, the ranger sent me to Trainer Lake, south of Fort Simpson. I had to bring empty fuel barrels back from a fire near there, along with other gear.

After a rather long day, I tied up for the night and walked to the local hotel where I ate supper and returned to my room. The next several days were much the same, as I continued flying empty barrels from Trainer Lake to Fort Simpson.

Fort Simpson is a rather small town, set in a vast wilderness area. There is a Hudson Bay store, post office, Royal Canadian Mounted Police headquarters, a hotel and restaurant and several large docks where riverboats and tugs tie up. Most of the supplies are brought in during the summer by boat, as the river freezes over each winter. I met some interesting people who called this northern settlement home, and I enjoyed observing their lifestyle.

My work was finished August 8th, and the forest ranger at Fort Simpson released me. Soon I had IBP gassed and was on course for Watson Lake. I flew direct, which took me a few miles south of Nahanni Butte, visible in the sky-blue weather. However, just west of this where the mountains began, we hit some severe turbulence, and I slowed down as the Beaver bucked and fought an unseen foe. Every so often I checked the wings to be sure they were still there and not separating, but the strong Beaver remained in one piece.

We crossed the Whitefish River, then the Beaver River and Tobally Lakes were visible straight ahead. I was over familiar territory now, and Larry Schnig's fishing camp was visible. The air turbulence had subsided somewhat, much to my relief.

Although I enjoyed trips to new areas, it was always nice to come home to Watson Lake (especially after many days on a freight haul), shower, change clothes and have a nice dinner at the log Watson Lake Hotel, which is located on the Alaska Highway near the sign post. It's a collection of highway and town signs from all over Canada and the USA. It was started by a homesick GI working on the Alaska Highway in about 1942.

I got one day off and caught up on my laundry and other things that needed to be done. I purchased some lake front property on Watson Lake from the Yukon government and put a trailer on it. It was across the bay from Watson Lake Flying Service seaplane base. Sometimes I canoe to work. I could rest at my home on the lake where there was no phone, and peace and quiet reigned supreme.

August 10th I had a trip to Chuck Hayward's camp on Little Dal Lake. The hunting season was in full swing. Chuck's area had some good Dall sheep rams, which are the trophy most hunters come up here for. His hunters also shot caribou and grizzly bears, but the sheep were the most sought-after trophy, and the hunts were very expensive. Chuck had a first-class outfit.

Little Dal Lake sits on a plateau about 5,600 feet above sea level, with the rugged Mackenzie Mountains rising in the east. It was a favorite of mine when the weather was decent; in bad weather, because of the high mountain passes, it could be very hazardous to my health. I was very careful and especially watchful in bad weather, as most of the valleys look alike, and it was easy to get turned around and lost while flying. A few years ago, on a return flight to Watson Lake, a Beaver crashed during bad weather on a high pass a few miles north of the Nahanni River, killing all on board.

The trip up and back took about five hours, including the loading and unloading. The flying time was about two hours each way. The weather was good and the trip uneventful. Dall sheep were visible on the grassy hillsides near Little Dal Lake, and the hunters I dropped off with Chuck were all smiles. They anticipated a good hunt and were probably dreaming about getting a world record Dall sheep.

The hunting season starts earlier here (about July 15) than in the areas south, because it freezes up around the end of September. The outfitters have to leave much earlier or take a chance of losing their horses, as it takes about two weeks to trail them from here to the nearest road.

The next few days involved trips closer to Watson Lake. I flew to Moodie and Twin Lakes, south of Watson Lake about 120 miles or so, for Frank Cooke and Sons outfitters, then made a trip to Eaglehead and another lake for George Dalziel.

On September 9, 1971 I began a memorable trip into Deadman's Valley that lasted for a couple weeks, flying men and supplies in from Fort Liard and Nahanni Butte to fight a forest fire.

Our crew by our Beech 18 CF-NCL at the Watson Lake Flying Service.
Left: Dave, Jim Thibaudreau, who flew the Beech 18, Stan Bridcut, Larry
Whitesitt, Jim Close, John Poiser, and kneeling is Wally Waulkonan,
engineer. Jim Thibaudreau was killed in this plane in 1975 during bad
weather with two hunters a short time after I left in the fall.

Watson Lakes Flying Service office. Hunters wait to get out to the hunting
camps in the bush.

The Red Beaver floatplane getting a rebuilt engine installed at our hanger at Watson Lake Airport

Chapter 5

DEADMAN'S VALLEY

We received a call from the Forest Service at Fort Liard in the Northwest Territories, requesting the Beaver to fly men and freight into Deadman's Valley to fight a forest fire. Because of limited resources, the remote fires are normally left to burn; however, they wanted to put this fire out as quickly as possible, because it was in the proposed Nahanni National Park area.

This was a new adventure for me, as it was my first flight into Headless Valley or, as it's called on my sectional chart, Deadman's Valley. Deadman's Valley is located just inside the Northwest Territories, in the southwest corner of this vast land. The mighty Mackenzie Mountains divide the Yukon and Northwest Territories and run in a northwesterly direction. Not far from here is the Arctic Circle, an imaginary line on the map which marks the zone where the sun does not set on at least one day of summer and does not rise on at least one day of winter.

The tree line, an area where it's too cold for trees to grow, cuts across the territories from the Mackenzie River delta in the northwest toward the Hudson Bay Coast in the southeast. North of the tree line are vast expanses of arctic tundra, large areas consisting of rock desert that is bare of vegetation except for a short period during the summer when tiny flowers bloom. The rest is mostly covered by grass-like plants, mosses and lichens that provide excellent grazing for herds of caribou and shaggy musk oxen. South of the tree line the tundra is mixed with scattered stands of stunted conifers. White birch, one of the few deciduous trees able to stand the cold, can be found in a few places. Because of the low rainfall and short summer, trees grow very slowly here.

The only really thick forests are south and west of Great Slave Lake in the Mackenzie River basin. Birch, spruce, balsam, jack pine, fir, tamarack and aspen are fairly common. The winters, though cold and very long, are dry and healthy. With spring comes an immediate transformation from ice and snow to an immense area of thousands of shallow lakes with no outlets. A few, however, are connected with river systems that empty into the sea.

Wildlife includes moose along the Mackenzie Valley, with grizzlies, black bear and Dall sheep in the western mountains. Small game, such as beaver, arctic foxes, muskrats and other furbearers is plentiful. Wood buffalo are found west and south of Great Slave Lake; north are the woodland caribou, which are larger than the barren ground caribou, live in small groups rather than in herds and don't migrate.

The great white Arctic wolves prey on the musk oxen and weaker caribou. On the coast you can find polar bears, whales and seals. Waterfowl such as geese, ducks and swans arrive for the summer breeding season, as do birds of prey, such as the snowy owl and peregrine falcon. The ptarmigan is one of the few birds that stay north; most of the rest migrate. I often saw them in my flights to Howard Pass, around the mining camp there.

The Yukon and Northwest Territories occupy almost 40 percent of Canadian land, yet this land holds less than one-half of one percent of the total population of Canada.

The South Nahanni River runs through Deadman's Valley. The Nahanni is a very dangerous river of whitewater, jagged rocks and swiftly changing channels and is reputed to be the most treacherous and fastest flowing river in North America, with an average speed of 12 knots. It has risen as much as seven feet in one hour after one of the vicious rain and wind storms common to this area has unleashed its fury.

The air was smooth, the 450 horsepower Pratt & Whitney radial engine roared reassuringly, and I trimmed the airplane level at about 7500 feet. There wasn't a road or any sign of man as we headed across the eastern part of the Yukon and then into the Northwest Territories.

It's a given time of reflection as I marvel at the Creator's handiwork from this vantage point. We're a tiny speck on this vast expanse of sky and earth.

This first season flying for Watson Lake Flying Service has been chuck full of new adventures, new firsts for me. It started out with a trip to Florida to pick up a float-equipped Beaver in Fort Meyers, Florida and fly it to the Yukon. I met some wonderful, warm and friendly people in the South who helped me in so many ways: people driving me to airports for fuel, a stranger in Memphis, Tennessee giving me his car to use overnight, and the waitresses saying "Honey" this and "Honey" that.

Then on August 5 I flew to Yellowknife, the capital of the Northwest Territories and later spent several days flying out of Fort Simpson on a fire. There were interesting trips with canoe parties into the fabled South Nahanni River, into the rugged Mackenzie Mountains to Little Dal Lake with sheep hunters and trips for Frank Cooke and Sons, outfitters in northern B.C. Now I was flying to a place I had heard so much about – Headless Valley – and would actually be living here until a fire was brought under control.

Leaving the Yukon in the red Beaver, I crossed into the Northwest Territories near the headwaters of Meilleur River, which flows into Deadman's Valley on a northeasterly direction. The Mackenzie Mountains began on the north side of the South Nahanni River. They are the most difficult mountains that I have ever navigated in, as the different valleys and mountains look almost identical, and it's easy to get turned around and lost. Several pilots and passengers have died in plane crashes here while flying these mountains in bad weather.

While I was excited to begin the new adventure and operate off the fabled South Nahanni River at Deadman's Valley, I also felt a certain reservation and some apprehension in the Mackenzie Mountains. Flying over the Funeral Range, which is just west of the valley, I noticed the mountains were barren of trees above 4,000 or 5,000 feet. They had a desolate look, much like mountains I'd seen in Arizona in the dry desert areas. The elevation of the valley is under 2,000 feet, according to the map.

Past the junction of the Meuilleur and Nahanni rivers a few miles downriver, I saw a cabin on the south side and some people camped nearby, directly across from where Prairie Creek enters the South Nahanni. I think it must be Albert Faille's old cabin. He was a noted explorer and an expert with the canoe. He came to this country in the '20s and stayed some 40 years.

Circling the camp, I checked the river for debris and rocks, picking out a clear channel and landed below the cabin into the current As I came off the step, the current slowed me down rapidly, and I had to use a fair amount of power to keep from being pushed backward. Maneuvering toward a makeshift dock, I slipped up alongside, and a native on the dock tied me down.

This was an Indian camp, and these Indians were of the Nahane Tribe, which means "people of the West." The Nahane form a major division of the Athapascan linguistic stock. They are located in northern B.C. and the Yukon Territory, between the coast range and Rocky Mountains, with some bands extending to the Mackenzie River.

The foreman, John, was there to greet me. He, the woman cook and the fire fighters were all local Indians. John was the only native who spoke English, so he quickly filled me in on what was happening and what I would be doing.

The fire had already burned a large area, and the government wanted to stop it as quickly as possible, because this area would be part of the Nahanni National Park; any scars would be visible for years to come. I would be working for the forest ranger at Fort Liard and Fort Simpson and John here at the fire camp headquarters where I would sleep in a tent.

John said, "Larry, you are to fly on to Fort Simpson and pick up some supplies and return to camp tomorrow." Before leaving, I checked out the camp. The log cabin was used as the cookhouse, and the men lived in tents set up near the cabin.

With some help from the natives I prepared to depart for Fort Simpson. A native held the Beaver to the dock after it was untied, until I could get in and start it up. The engine started easily, the native pushed me out a bit and I began preparation for takeoff.

I enjoy working rivers; it's a real challenge and keeps me on my toes. I get a lot of satisfaction from successfully completing a tough river operation without mishap. So far I'd been fortunate and had no accidents on rivers, although a few hairy times I came close to losing it. Currents, contrary winds, rocks and shallow waters in silty, murky rivers where the visibility is only a few inches are some of the hazards that can put you out of commission quickly, wrecking your plane and maybe taking your life.

Once on the raging Keel River in the Northwest Territories I was turned loose before I could get the Beaver started. Whitewater rapids and large ugly rocks were waiting to wreck me a short distance downstream. If the old reliable 450-horsepower R-985 had coughed a few times before starting, the Beaver would have been lost – and perhaps me, as well. Fortunately it started quickly, averting a disaster.

My first takeoff from Headless Valley was safely accomplished, and I set course for Fort Simpson 110 miles northeast. Flying over the first canyon I noticed the canyon walls seemed to rise straight up from the river; I thought I might fly low through the canyon at a later date and get a better look. Next I noticed Kraus's cabin on the south side of the river east of the canyon, with hot springs behind the cabin about 100 yards or so.

Soon the valley widened out, and Nahanni Butte was visible under my starboard wing. Just east of this Indian village the country flattened out as far as I could see, and the mighty Mackenzie Mountains slipped slowly behind.

Fort Simpson is located on an island at the junction of the Liard and Mackenzie rivers. The first fort here, Fort of the Forks, was established by the Northwest Company in 1804. In 1821 the Hudson Bay Company built a post here, and it was named for George Simpson, the Hudson Bay Company governor.

Fort Simpson was visible at last. Since I had been here earlier this season, the river and docks were familiar. A normal final approach (after first circling to look for debris at my proposed landing site) at 80 mph indicated round out, landing attitude and a smooth landing was accomplished. Sometimes it seemed that when there was an audience watching and I tried hard to impress someone, I bounced! But after flying the Beaver for a while, you get fairly proficient and can usually set it down gently.

After tying up, I walked to the District Ranger's headquarters, about a quarter mile away. It was getting late in the day, so I decided to overnight and return to Deadman's Valley with men and supplies the next day. I arranged dinner at the restaurant and another overnight stay at the hotel. One nice thing about working for the Forest Service was that I got my board and room in addition to my base pay and mileage, or hourly rate, whichever applied. They were nice to work for, and it was satisfying to know I was able to be a part of a worthwhile effort to protect a future national park from going up in smoke.

After a good night's sleep and breakfast, I loaded men and supplies into the Beaver and made an early departure off the river. Fort Simpson slipped behind, and I retraced my route over now-familiar country.

The flight back took about one hour. Landing against the current, I noticed some natives walking to the pole dock to give me a hand. I always appreciated that on a river; jumping out alone to tie down can be tricky in a strong current.

I soon began flying to Nahanni Butte, picking up freight and then flying back to camp. A DC-3 was flying in loads of supplies to the airstrip at the village of Nahanni Butte The freight was then brought down to the river, where it was loaded onto the Beaver for the flight to Deadman's Valley.

My work was cut out for me. It's only 40 air miles, which meant most of my time was loading and unloading with a 25-minute break of flying in between. Much of the freight consisted of 45-gallon drums of fuel for the helicopters that freighted men and supplies out of our camp at Deadman's Valley to the fire. I usually carried three drums in the Beaver. I always tied them down with ropes. If they slid back while I was in the air, the center of gravity would be too far aft. That happened to one pilot and was fatal.

When I landed back at camp, John, the foreman, informed me, "The other pilot never ties down the drums in his Beaver, but of course he probably knows his airplane better than you do." I didn't say anything, but that "other pilot" had wrecked several airplanes and was on the careless side, probably lucky to be alive. In any case, I had nothing to prove and just wanted to safely get this job completed with no damage to the airplane or pilot.

On September 15 I flew to Fort Liard then to Fort Simpson and back to Fort Liard to overnight. The flights went well, as usual with the red Beaver. Returning to Fort Liard from Fort Simpson, I was in a good mood. I would be staying in Fort Liard overnight for the first time and would have a chance to look around and do some sightseeing at the Indian settlement. In the fall the natives from the outlying villages and camps boarded their children at Fort Simpson, where the children attended school. A young and very beautiful Indian woman took care of them in a large dorm-like building.

While growing up in Spokane, Washington in the 1940s I lived a couple of houses away from the chief of the Coeur d'Alene Indians, Chief Joseph Seltice. He was the last Chief of the Coeud d'Alenes. He was a kind man and his grandchildren adored him. He was an engineer and his brother was a pharmacist. He had three grandchildren my age living with him. They were all girls, and we were good buddies. I've always had special feelings since then for Native Americans. I remember these girls – Evonne, Doty and Adrianna – who would show me their skin and say, "See, people don't like us because our skin is not the same as yours." We were in grade school then. I told them, "You're my friends, and to me you are no different than anyone else." My buddies would tease me, but to me the Indian girls were very special friends. We spent much time together playing games and having a good time growing up together.

One day at Nahanni Butte I was watching the DC-3 bring in another load of supplies. When the captain shut off the engines a young, pretty, smiling French girl named Sheila climbed down from the DC-3. I learned she was a French photographer and freelance writer wanting to do an article on Deadman's Valley. I flew Sheila into our camp, and she stayed in the cookhouse with the Indian woman cook. Sheila stayed three days writing and taking photos and then left.

A few months later Sheila sent a letter from South America with slides that she had taken of the Beaver. I still have them. The one I use for a business card is me just taking off the Nahanni in the red Beaver IBP. She was so good-looking that she was probably able to hitch free rides, much as she did with the pilot on the DC-3 and with me. She was full of life and enjoyed her visit in the wilderness very much.

Jim was driving through the Yukon on the Alaska Highway and was stopped because of tremendous forest fires burning throughout the territories. He readily agreed to help fight a forest fire and was flown into this camp before I arrived. Jim was from back East, probably in his twenties, a long-haired hippy type. I soon found out he was an okay guy, and I enjoyed his company.

At night we had a ritual of sitting around the campfire until the wee hours of the morning, watching the northern lights, talking about the States, the North, or just listening to the night sounds of the river and bush. Those nights along the banks of the Nahanni River were pleasant, satisfying times.

The campsite and the area close by was wild and beautiful; the fall colors were magnificent along the river. The top half of the mountains, a short distance away, were bare looking, but it was pleasant on the river here by camp.

Besides hauling freight from Nahanni Butte to Deadman's Valley almost daily, I made several trips to Fort Liard and Fort Simpson. Those longer trips were a welcome relief from the short freight hauls.

One overcast day I had several trips from the airstrip at Nahanni Butte to our camp. I had been flying direct, a short cut across some ridges just south of the first canyon, to save time. The ceiling had been dropping, but I didn't really want to fly through the windy, narrow first canyon. I saw some daylight between the clouds and the ridge, so I decided to take that route again.

The clouds enveloped me as I started to fly over the ridge; I could see only the inside of a white cloud. I was above the valley, mountains on the other side, no navigation aids. I shouted, "Oh God," thinking I had mere seconds before I crashed into a mountainside. I figured this was it, and that I would soon be buying the farm for good! Split second terror!!! A helpless feeling. There was a slight drop in elevation ahead, so I maintained the heading and altitude. I slid down the window on my door and stuck my head out, trying to see the ground.

The fall-colored tops of trees flashed red and orange periodically. I felt temporary relief when I broke through the clouds a couple of times, only to be plunged back into whiteness. When I finally broke through to clear air, the relief was one of joy, of new life – another chance to live. Fortune once again smiled on me. I'm not sure why. Others have not been so fortunate here in the Mackenzie Mountains. I was thankful to God for letting me live. That was the last time I took the shortcut; from then on I flew through the narrow first canyon where the visibility was good.

I left Headless Valley for Fort Liard on September 25 with men and gear. The fire was out, and my job was finished here. I unloaded, fueled up and taxied out into the Liard River. The roar of the engine drowned out all sounds as I took off upstream to the south. The floats left the water, and Fort Liard disappeared behind the red Beaver.

I had a souvenir of this sojourn – a beautiful pair of moose moccasins with intricate beadwork, made by a native woman in Nahanni Butte. My size 13 feet fit perfectly into the custom-made moccasins. Additionally, I had many adventures to relive in my mind, two beautiful women I met and a few more grey hairs caused by a close call with death in Deadman's Valley. My memories were mostly pleasant ones, of natives living in the bush, dried moose meat in the sun, of new country, new friends and a safe return of the red Beaver and this grateful pilot to Watson Lake.

The flight back to Watson was about 190 miles. The weather was good, and I was glad to be on course to a hot shower, old friends and maybe dinner at the Watson Lake Hotel. After what seemed like a long trip, Watson Lake finally came into view. I approached from the east and let down over the trees north of the base. I came off the step at the point of land near the seaplane base and taxied to the dock. After leaning the mixture, the engine quit, switches off and I stepped off the float to tie IBP to the dock. A memorable trip safely completed, now I looked forward to a few nights in my own bed. I left on September 9, 1971 and was back September 25, safe and sound. In the next few days I flew into Meeting Lake with IBP and to the Turnagain River and back to Watson Lake, then to Skook's Ranch on the Kechika River.

I climbed into IBP on September 30 for the last trip of the season. I tried to make a charter flight, but the weather was bad.

This is a photo of the largest recorded moose shot in Canada by the Keel River in the Northwest Territory.

CHAPTER 6

RESCUING HORSES ON
THE NAHANNI WITH SCOTT

A s I flew back to Watson Lake on CPA, I reflected on events of the winter just past. Now I looked forward to a new season of flying the bush renewing friendships and, of course, making some money. The pilots at Watson Lake Flying Service were well paid. We had a substantial base salary, as well as a mileage rate, which doubled after 10,000 miles in any given month.

The Boeing 737 stopped at Prince George, Fort John, Fort Nelson; now it was on course to Watson Lake, my home in the Yukon Territory. This was my fourth season in this vast land, and as we got close to our destination I saw familiar landmarks below: the Alaska Highway, the Liard River, the Rocky Mountains and countless unnamed wilderness lakes.

Flying around the edge of Watson Lake, we turned final. The wheels touched with a solid thump, the brakes caught, and we rapidly slowed on the short runway. Across the lake from the end of the runway lay a World War II bomber in shallow water near the shore. It took off on an almost empty tank and ran dry shortly after takeoff. The bomber lay in the lake bottom as a less on to pilots: always check and switch to the fullest gas tank before takeoff.

Another rule I followed rigidly was to never pilot an airplane after drinking. I always had a night of sleep before piloting an airplane, even after one drink. Alcohol reduces the amount of oxygen your system has, and as you gain altitude, which also deprives your system of oxygen, the effect can be deadly. Your coordination is off, and your judgment and depth perception are adversely affected.

Sometimes when I was flying Indians to a hunting camp and they were drunk or had one big hangover and started to give me a bad time, I would climb to 7,000 feet or so. The effect of less oxygen at such an altitude, combined with their rich alcohol-soaked blood, would cause them to pass out. When they knew they were going out for the season guiding, they would get drunk at their village and then hide. We would go down, find them, pour them into the company pickup, then pour them into the Beaver. Once out in the bush they were excellent guides, after they had some time to sober up.

One of the pilots I flew with would come to work after an all-night drunk, pour himself into the pilot's seat with no sleep and fly away. I noticed he was very careless; he didn't tie down the 45-gallon drums in the airplane to keep them from sliding to the back of the plane. I didn't like to fly the same Beaver he had flown, not knowing what he might have done. He was a poor pilot and a danger to himself and anyone he flew. Another pilot who flew helicopters would take a drink of whiskey before flying, which really surprised me; he was an older man, a man I thought should have known better.

As I walked off the plane, the same small terminal building and familiar faces greeted me. It felt good to be back north from "the outside," as we referred to a trip beyond the Yukon.

Between the middle of May and early June the ice leaves Watson Lake. One year it was about June 15 before the ice left and we could begin flying off the lake. Some of the higher lakes don't shed their ice until July or August, but this June the lakes and rivers in the lower valley were open, and we began our busy season once again. Spring comes quickly to the north. Almost overnight it seems everything is in bloom. Growth is rapid because of the long days of sunlight – it is still daylight at midnight.

Before we actually got the planes on floats and in the water, there was always work to be done scraping floats, fixing leaky compartments and then painting them. Once the floats were finished and attached to the planes, we hauled them from the airport on a trailer to a nearby launching area close to the airport. We test flew them, then returned for another season at our seaplane base located on the east end of Watson Lake.

It was good to be flying again this sunny day of June 5, 1972. I taxied out in our Cessna 185 YIG, prepared to do a few circuits and landings to get back in the swing of things. Run up, full power applied and the Cessna quickly got on the step and in the air with just the company check pilot and me. A few landings to get the feel once again of a float plane and I was prepared to begin another season flying prospectors, hunters, guides, canoe parties and, of course, fire patrol. The season at this time started out slowly but would soon be in full swing. Just getting enough sleep would become a problem.

My first charter flight was in my favorite airplane, the red Beaver CF-IBP on June 8. I flew two passengers to North Lake and logged 2.2 hours.

I obtained a lake lot on Watson Lake from the Yukon government and would be able to obtain title when I put in $2,000 in improvements. I purchased a small trailer and set it up on the property, and Scott and I stayed in it. Scott and I ran, spent as much time together as possible, and I took him on as many trips as I could. He spent a lot of time around airplanes and the men of the North – prospectors, hunters, trappers, truckers – and was growing up in a man's world. Sometimes he stayed in the bush for several days at a mining camp and did some serious fishing. His favorite part was the camp cooking; their delicious meals of steak and pie, a wonderful treat compared to my cooking.

The mosquitoes were fierce once you stepped outside, but it was nice to have my own place to come home to after a long day flying. Sometimes I canoed from my place to the base, which was about 15 minutes away.

June 10 I prepared my Beaver for a flight to Skook Davidson's Ranch on the Kechika River in the Rocky Mountain Trench. Skook was a living legend, a symbol of a passing era in this country. His ranch was about 110 miles southeast of Watson Lake in a wilderness area without roads or electricity. He had no neighbors for about a hundred miles, except for a few outfitters during the hunting season.

After fueling IBP and doing a thorough preflight check, I began loading sacks of horse feed. I taxied toward the bay at the south end of the lake, and within 30 seconds we were off the water. Heading south, I soon passed over downtown Watson Lake and continued climbing as the Liard River passed under my wings.

One of Frank Cook's hunting camps on Scoop Lake west of the Kechika River came into sight. Frank was a first-class outfitter and guide – one of my favorites to fly for. He had one of the finest stone sheep areas in the country, and record-class heads were common in his area. Skook's place was 20 miles beyond Frank's.

Soon Skook's ranch and landing site on the Kechika River came into view. I circled, looking for river debris before making my final approach. I landed into the current and was kept busy working the plane against the current toward a tie-up spot nudged into the beach.

Skook waited stoically in a horse-drawn wagon about 20 feet away. He was up in years, maybe close to 80, but still solidly built. He had arthritis, which had slowed him down some and made walking difficult, so he didn't get off the wagon. I unloaded the horse feed and groceries onto the bank and then carried it to the wagon. Skook said hello but little else as I loaded his wagon. He watched me walk to the Beaver and shove off into the current. I was glad to meet this silent, living legend of the North. I was soon in the air, and Skook and his wagon disappeared behind. It was a privilege to know this man and to be able to fly into his isolated world.

One day I heard that Dennis Ball had crashed in the float-equipped Otter. The story I heard from another pilot, a friend of Dennis's, was the following: Dennis radioed in to B.C. Yukon's flight office that he was following Lafferty Creek, on course to a lake in the Mackenzie Mountains with six 45-gallon drums of fuel and one passenger to a mining camp. "I'll just stick my nose in and take a look. If the weather's not good, I'll return to the base camp and do some fishing." That was the last transmission heard. Sid Baird left a short while later to search for Dennis in the jet ranger helicopter. It looked like Dennis took a wrong turn up a blind canyon, tried to make a 180 and then crashed into a mountainside, killing himself and his passenger.

I booked another trip with horse feed, saddles and gas to the Turnagain River, into Earl Boose's hunting camp about 80 miles south. Earl and Marge, his wife, ran a good camp and were well known in the guiding and outfitting business. The trip was uneventful, except for the final approach and landing on a tricky, shallow river that kept me on my toes, as usual.

One cardinal sin was forgetting the mail. The isolated camps looked forward with a passion to letters from the outside. Pity the poor bush pilot who forgot it – which on occasion had been my bad fortune.

The big game hunting camp was nestled in a beautiful setting on the north side of the river. Coffee and pie were a pleasant treat while the isolated campers asked questions about various events, what people were doing, how Jim and Stan were doing and world news. They helped by holding the Beaver until it started. Then the guys swung my tail around so I was headed downstream for takeoff, as there were obstructions upstream. I had to be careful on the river's series of turns, rocks and shallow water.

Early in July I prepared for an interesting journey to the South Nahanni River. We had received an emergency call earlier from one of Chuck Hayward's guides. One guide had been swimming his horse across the Nahanni River when the horse had drowned underneath him. The rawboned cowboy guide, a non-swimmer, was trapped on a sandbar in the middle of the river. The Nahanni was in flood stage and rising. We were asked to send the plane immediately, as the life of the guide was in danger.

Jon Poizer, one of our pilots, left with the Super Cub. He successfully picked up the guide and took him to an island on the river to which the rest of the guides and horses had first swum.

Jim Close said, "Larry, fly up to Little Dal Lake near where Chuck has his main hunting camp. Pick up Chuck and fly him to the group stranded on the island. See what can be done to get the rest of the horses across the river." This was a crucial time for Chuck. He had to have his camp and horses ready for the first Dall sheep Hunt starting July 15. From where they were stranded, it would take two weeks of steady riding to get to camp.

Scott was with me, as I decided it would be a good trip to take him on. We had a light load, and the Beaver climbed quickly north toward Little Dal Lake. With good weather the trip was 220 miles. As I often did, I let Scott have the controls so that he built up some more co-pilot time.

We flew parallel to the Hyland River, and before long we could see the landmark high glacier peaks above Glacier Lake. We passed over the South Nahanni River just north of Glacier Lake at about 8,000 feet. Little Dal Lake lay about another 80 miles over these rugged Mackenzie Mountains. The valleys and peaks looked so much alike that I always concentrated closely and kept a map handy to make sure I was on course.

"Scott, it looks like we're about there," I said as the blue speck of Little Dal Lake appeared. I flew over Chuck's camp first and then circled the lake in a descending turn. We touched down a few hundred feet from shore. The Beaver settled into the water after a few bounces, something I tried not to do in front of a client – but such is life. We unloaded a few things for Chuck's camp and readied for the flight to the stranded guides and horses with Chuck on board.

After 80 miles we spotted some horses on a quarter-mile long island. I circled the raging river, looking for logs and debris and found a spot that appeared clear. We touched down into the current, landing in a westerly direction. The current was swift, and I needed plenty of power just to keep from going backwards. Working into the current, I eased the Beaver toward shore where the guides were standing, ready to secure the plane. I was glad for their help to heel the back of the floats onto the beach and securely tie the Beaver to some small trees.

We began constructing a breastwork of logs and driftwood from shore. We hoped we could drive the horses into the river and to the shore on the north side; the horses had other ideas. Because the river was shallow by the island, they walked around the breastwork and back onto the east side of the island. We fired guns and chased horses up and down the island.

Chuck decided to fly in a boat and motor. He hoped to pull the lead horses across the river so that the others would follow. He and I flew to Cantung (Tungsten), a mining town about 50 miles west, for an aluminum boat and motor. We tied it securely and returned to the island.

Chuck and one guide pulled one horse behind the boat stern into the water. Once in deep water, the horse swam behind the boat through the swollen waters. On the other side, the propeller hit bottom and broke. Since the boat would not make it back on its own power, I pulled it back with the Beaver.

It was late. Nothing more could be done, so we prepared to spend the night on the island. We all sat around the campfire telling stories before turning in for the night. Scott and I slept in the Beaver.

Chuck decided to fly back to Cantung the next morning. A shop there was able to fix the propeller, but we lost another several hours flying to Cantung, fixing the propeller and flying back.

Chuck finally made a couple of successful trips getting horses across the river and all seemed to be going well. Suddenly, near the other shore the boat capsized. Chuck and the guide were swept rapidly downstream. A sweeper, a downed tree extending into the swirling water, saved their lives. After a fierce struggle with the current pulling at them and the weight of their wet clothes, they dragged themselves up the tree and onto the shore.

The boat and motor were lost. Once again I cranked up the Beaver and taxied from the island to pick up the two men. The horse they were pulling when the boat capsized made it safely to the far shore.

Darell Nelson, who was in the process of buying Chuck's outfit, was one of the men stranded on the island. "When I saw the Beaver fly over, it was like the angel of deliverance," he said. Darell lost 25 pounds on that trek.

Now that a few of the lead horses were on the other side of the river, the rest of the horses allowed us to drive them into the water and across. After a broken propeller, a sunken boat and a near drowning, the horses and guides were safely across. Scott and I left for home with a new respect for the raging South Nahanni River, which even at this late date was still in flood stage.

It was July 8, and the fire season was upon us again. I had a forest ranger as co-pilot and was flying our Twin Apache CF-KXL on a long patrol. The fire danger was high. It was a treat to fly a Twin once in awhile; it was faster, quieter and handled more like an executive ship. The Beaver was still my favorite, but it was fun to get time in other types. July 16 I flew our Twin Beach 18 into Wasson Lake on a fire.

On another trip a few days later I flew some mining people into Telegraph Creek, an old mining community from the past century's gold rush days. Telegraph Creek sits on a high ridge above the Stikine River. I landed the Beaver above the town on Sawmill Lake.

The store owner, Doug Blanchard, met us at the lake and gave us a ride to this tiny community. He owned one of the two stores; the other was owned by Hudson Bay Company. Telegraph Creek was laid-back and peaceful – no hurry, just an easy, slow pace. I was fortunate to stay overnight so had a chance to walk around and get a feel of Telegraph Creek's rich history. Across the town and up the hill lived the Tahltan Indians in their small houses – some painted blue and red and some with just weather-beaten boards. The Indian cemetery nearby still had the little painted spirit houses over the graves, an old Indian custom.

The warm, long lazy summer days and the slow pace of the locals in Telegraph Creek would, I always thought, make this an ideal place to spend a vacation, to unwind and just enjoy. Telegraph Creek was to become one of my favorite destinations and a place I visited many times in the years ahead.

At an early age I had been an avid reader of stories about the Klondike gold rush and stories of the North – Telegraph Creek, Dawson City, the Yukon River. Robert Service's poems and Jack London's stories were all vivid in my mind. Those boyhood hours of reading made my in-person visits to this land even more enjoyable. The flight back to Watson Lake was pleasant, as I thought of this unique village so rich in history.

Another favorite place of mine, Atlin, British Columbia, was one of my destinations in the red Beaver CF-IBP. A few days later, some mining officials had booked to Atlin, then to Whitehorse with a return to Watson Lake, a flight of just over seven flying hours.

Atlin town site had the most beautiful setting I had ever seen in my travels up north. It sits on the east side of Atlin Lake. This clean, clear 90-mile-long lake is the largest natural lake in British Columbia and is about 900 feet deep. Lake herring, whitefish, Arctic grayling, ling cod and lake trout make their homes in these waters. Glaciers rise above the lake to the west. Birch Mountain, the tallest island mountain in a freshwater lake in the world, is on Teresa Island.

Gold was discovered here in 1898 by Fritz Miller, a German immigrant, and Kerry McLaren, a Nova Scotian. This area is rich in history in its own right, as well as being located along the Klondikers' route to Dawson City.

The flight from Watson Lake to Atlin was about 170 air miles. The course paralleled the Alaska Highway for a while, although it was many miles south and crossed the southern tip of Teslin Lake. It was a nice flight, the weather was good and Atlin was visible many miles ahead. In the clear air it looked like a sleepy, almost deserted, small town next to the huge lake. We tied up at the dock near the town site, and my passengers took care of their business.

After lunch we departed for Whitehorse, the capitol of the Yukon, a 45-minute flight to the northwest over some spectacular scenery. Whitehorse became the capitol of the Yukon in 1953 after the territorial government was moved from Dawson City. From a village of less than 500, it grew to over 20,000 as people poured into town to commence building the Alaskan Highway in 1942. It's a regional service center outlet for Yukon communities.

We landed on the fabled Yukon River behind a dam close to the city. My passengers got a ride into town from the seaplane docks on the river. After fueling I taxied into the river, flaps trim, full power. With no load the red Beaver seemed to leap on the step. We were in the air in a few short seconds and climbing rapidly on our easterly course to our home base at Watson Lake. The flight course took us by the north end of Marsh Lake and Teslin Lake. The community of Teslin on the east side of the lake began around 1903 with the founding of a trading post serving the nomadic Teslinegit Indians. About 400 people lived here now.

Soon we were flying over the Cassier Mountains and over Meister Lake. It was only 60 miles to home, a hot shower, supper and a rest after seven hours with the constant roar of the radial engine numbing my ears and body. After landing it was just nice to get away from the noisy engine and walk along the quiet lakeshore.

It was July 15 and the season was passing quickly as I prepared IBP for a supply and mail run into Broken Bit on the Kechika River for Frank Cook, the outfitter. It was about 110 miles down the Rocky Mountain trench, close to one hour flying time. After landing and unloading I had one side trip before returning to Watson Lake. The trip was routine, with no problem landing on the river, the flight home smooth.

An accident on the Alaska Highway with some critically injured people brought a call for a couple of airplanes from our company to fly the injured from Watson Lake to Whitehorse immediately. It was night and we were not normally allowed to fly floats after dark. Because of the emergency situation we were allowed to make that trip. It was midsummer, and the days were getting shorter, but in the land of the midnight sun there was still enough light to fly visually.

We loaded one patient and a nurse who would monitor the patient while I flew my Beaver IBP. We were soon on course for Whitehorse. Jim Thibaudeau was flying a couple of injured patients and another nurse in his Beech 18 He too left the lake, heading for Whitehorse. The air was relatively smooth, the flight uneventful. My male patient groaned and seemed to be seriously injured and in much pain. The nurse closely watched and tried to make him as comfortable as possible.

Whitehorse had the only real hospital in the Yukon Territory. Watson Lake had a nursing station with about seven nurses and a doctor from England by the name of Wigby. The nursing station didn't have the facilities to take care of seriously injured patients, so they were usually flown to Whitehorse by Watson Lake Flying Service.

We arrived over the Yukon River near Whitehorse at about four in the morning after a flight of 240 miles over a remote wilderness area. We landed on the Yukon River in our floatplane. A waiting ambulance whisked the patient to the Whitehorse Hospital. I surely hoped he made it.

Jim and I and the two nurses had breakfast at Whitehorse before going back to Watson Lake. I left first in IBP and was flying merrily along when Jim pulled up beside my left wing, in formation for a few minutes and then passed me. The Beech 18 was a little faster than the Beaver. We arrived back at Watson Lake about 8 a.m. ready for another busy day.

One day I was enjoying coffee and conversation with Dr. Wigby. The good doctor had thick grey hair, bushy eyebrows and an ever-present serious look. In spite of appearances, he was a neat guy and very interesting to talk to. One of his favorite topics was flying. Although he had logged 70 hours of dual flying instruction, his solo time was zero. To date no instructor had felt comfortable turning him loose for his first solo, but Dr. Wigby's enthusiasm for flying was still very evident.

A canoe party needed a doctor on the Nahanni River; one of the party had a dislocated shoulder. Dr. Wigby and I left from Watson Lake and located the group after about an hour's flight. The man with the dislocated shoulder was in pain, and his injured shoulder was at an angle much lower than the other shoulder. Dr. Wigby put his knee in the man's back, his hands on his shoulder and gave a quick hard pull. The shoulder popped into place, and we left for Watson Lake. Dr. Wigby didn't believe in Canada's program of socialized medicine and refused to pay his premiums. He was occasionally jailed for his beliefs. I liked this man!

Early morning flights were a special treat, so often I was one of the first pilots on the lake and in the air. My destination one special day was a flight to a mining camp on Provinger Lake a few miles south of the Turnagain River. After my preflight check I pointed my craft down the lake, full power and we were airborne within seconds in the thick, cool air. The light before sunrise had a special quality. The valleys were still dark, without form, with only a faint light to the east over the Rocky Mountains. As I slipped smoothly through the clear air, a special early morning feeling of being the only one in this visible sky, of peace, of oneness with God and His creation, came over me. The steady drone of the engine, with wings attached to my back, made my world secure. Soaring like an eagle, looking down upon this untouched wilderness, gave me a feeling unlike anything else in life. Peaceful, alive, my world was here; it was perfect at this moment.

The advancing dawn brightened the sky, and the valley became alive. Trees, flowing rivers and meadows revealed themselves; the world below took form. Flying near the Turnagain River at 8,000 feet I began playing a game with the pure white cumulus tops, soaring in and around the valleys and peaks of these early morning giants of the sky. The air was still smooth as we danced with the clouds – alone, at peace with this early morning once-in-a-lifetime place, time and form.

My favorite poem was written by John Magee, an American pilot who lost his life in an air battle in World War II. It describes something close to what I felt as I soared in around these white mountains of clouds.

High Flight

Oh, I have slipped the surly bonds of earth
And danced the skies on laughter-silvered wings.
Sunward I've climbed, and joined the tumbling mirth
Of sun-split clouds – and done a hundred things
You have not dreamed of – wheeled and soared and swung
High in the sunlit silence. Hovering there
I've chased the shouting wind along, and flung
My eager craft through footless halls of air.
Up, up the long, delirious, burning blue
I've topped the windswept heights with easy grace

Where never lark, or even eagle flew –
And, while with silent, lifting mind I've trod
The high untrespassed sanctity of space,
Put out my hand and touched the face of God.

This early morning flight and once-in-a-lifetime experience was seared in my mind. In later years I often relived this most special time when I soared my craft in and around the high mountains of white clouds.

Several days later Jim Close told me that I would be flying the body of a man recently killed on the Alaska Highway. Loading a dead man in a body bag onto the Beaver was a strange experience. The front seat next to me was removed, and the body was beside me on the floor. The friend who was not injured in the accident sat in the back of the red Beaver. It was strange to glance from time to time at the bag on the floor beside me – a bag that carried the remains of a man who until a short time before was alive and driving down the highway. At Whitehorse we landed on the Yukon River and were met by a hearse and two men who helped unload the body. My trip back to Watson Lake gave me a chance to reflect and to appreciate life.

The vastness and beauty of this country continued to excite me as I flew into new areas and experienced firsthand the thrill of landing on a new river or lake. Each trip was different; adventures were many. I recorded many scenes with my camera, in my journal and in my mind.

On the last day of July, I prepared IBP for a trip into Glacier Lake, just south of the Nahanni River at the bottom of some impressive peaks surrounded by glaciers. The tallest peak was called Mt. Sir James MacBrien, at 9,062 feet. My passengers, a group of mountain climbers, were eager to get going. We headed north from Watson Lake on a trip of 145 miles. The steady drone of the engine almost put me to sleep, but after an hour and ten minutes we caught sight of the green spot, which was Glacier Lake. I made a lazy circle over the lake.

There was no wind; we had what was called a glassy water condition. Proper depth perception over glassy water is impossible. Many seaplane pilots have ended their careers under such conditions. I began a long approach, with flaps, over the trees at the east end heading west, flying low. I set up the Beaver in a landing attitude with power at about 100 to 200 feet per minute descent and continued this until we touched down. Often a pilot under these conditions thinks he is close to the water, rounds out and stalls 50 feet or so above the water with disastrous results. Another technique is to land near some weeds or close to shore, using the shoreline as a reference for depth, but you must always use extreme care.

After unloading the mountain climbers on the northwest shore, we took off toward the south and followed the west side of the mountains closely, getting a nice updraft. As I looked at the glaciers and mountain peaks that I soon surmounted, I wondered what would make these people climb for days to get to the top. The climbers, Glacier Lake and the ice fields were soon behind as I continued south to Watson Lake.

The rest of the season went rapidly. We flew into Frank Cook's camps, Moodie Colt, Scoop and Denetiah Lakes on a fairly regular basis, as well as flights for other outfitters, fishermen, prospectors and forestry officials.

September 26 I tied up the red Beaver after my last flight of the season to Whitefish Lake. I said my farewells and ended another season.

I flew down to Vancouver, B.C. and purchased a new 1972 blue four-door Volvo that would log many trips over the Alaska Highway in the coming years. It proved to be a rugged and reliable car and a favorite of mine.

I continued the running program I had started in the late 1960s while working at Omineca Air Service in B.C. On the last day of 1972 I ran two miles. My journal entry that day read, "Simplicity=key to happiness."

Chuck Hayward is in the boat with a hunting guide pulling these horses across the South Nahanni River. Just after Larry took this photo the boat capsized and was lost. Chuck and the guide were able to swim to the far north bank. I taxied the Beaver across and picked them up. They were soaked, but not injured, "a close call".

We flew a boat on top of the float and outboard motor to the South Nahanni River on a mission to rescue horses with Chuck Hayward, a big game hunting guide.

Little Dal Lake, Northwest Territories where Larry and Scott picked up the outfitter, Chuck Hayward and flew him to the South Nahanni River to rescue horses trapped on an island.

Virginia Falls (twice as high as Niagra Falls) on the South Nahanni river Northwest Territories near the place where Scott and Larry flew Chuck Hayward to. I would land just above the falls past the first bend on the left side of the river. This area by the falls later became part of Nahanni National Park, 2-1/2 times the size of Yellowstone National Park. Larry and Scott once flew park officials to the falls who were mapping out the area that later became part of the Nahanni National Park.

Chapter 7

SCOTT'S FLIGHT TO ALMOST LAKE

On April 8, 1973 after a preflight walk around the airplane, I strapped myself into the 150-horsepower Decathlon and began an aerobatic course with a World War II Air Force fighter pilot as the instructor. John owned the plane, and I figured he wouldn't do anything that was unsafe. However, we both had parachutes, just in case. The Decathlon had an inverted system that enabled you to fly upside down without the engine quitting. It was sturdily built for both negative and positive G's.

We headed over Lake Sammamish where I practiced stalls, loops, rolls, spirals and hammerhead stalls for .8 hours, which was about all I wanted for the first lesson. Three more lessons of .8 hours and a final one of 1.2 hours completed the course of barrel rolls, slow rolls, Immelmans, inverted flight, snap rolls, Cuban eights and the ultimate – at least for me – an outside loop.

Rolling over inverted, trying to reach 165 mph before beginning the climb to the top of the loop (and then the fun began!), stick forward and we were going straight down. Continuous forward pressure on the stick was imperative in order to finish the bottom side of the loop before the speed built up too greatly, causing structural failure. As we continued to go under on the bottom side of the loop to the level inverted position, I rolled the airplane right side up and finished our loop. I'm sure I wouldn't have won a contest, but I did successfully complete an outside loop – probably the only one I'll ever do. It is really uncomfortable pulling negative G's; you feel like you are going to leave your seat and fly out into space while puking your guts out.

It was interesting to fly upside down and to recover from unusual altitudes. It was a lot of fun to loop and roll through the sky and to open a new dimension of flying! Inverted, all the controls are reversed and everything is done opposite. To raise the nose, increasing the angle of attack, you use forward pressure.

John told me an interesting story about the German pilots of World War II. He said they all flew gliders first, before flying a power plane. Flying a glider, using the basic stick and rudder is what he thinks made them exceptional pilots. Many German pilots shot down hundreds of planes. John said whenever a student of his had problems flying a power plane, all he had to do was get him in a glider for some dual, and the problems would be resolved.

May 3rd I packed my bags, loaded the car and headed north once again. The next day I stopped at Prince George to pick up Scott, and we went to Chetwyn, B.C. where we stopped for the night. We spent the next night at Liard Hot Springs where we soaked in the steaming mineral-laden pools and arrived May 6th at Watson Lake. It was so nice to have Scott along, even though the next day I had to put him on a plane back to Prince George so he could finish out the school year, but I knew he would return in June to spend the summer with me. Kathy and I were divorced after 12 years of marriage, and she and Scott moved to Prince George where Scott attended school. Kathy was a good wife and a wonderful mother to Scott.

The long days of sunshine were back, and it was a beautiful, warm day in May of 1973. We were working daily now on floats, sanding, repairing and painting them in preparation for another busy season. The aspen trees surrounding the lake were clothed in their spring greenery, and the ground was covered with a rich carpet of new growth. Spring came almost overnight, a spectacular transformation.

The frostless growing season in the Yukon is short, but it balances out with almost continuous sunlight during June, July and August. Agriculture is hurt more from lack of moisture than from the frost. Dense forests cover an area in the southeast portion of the Yukon, thinning gradually toward the west and north. The tree line is north of the Arctic Circle in the Yukon; white spruce is the most common tree, together with lodge pole pine, aspen, larch, alpine fir and black spruce. Farther north it's mostly black spruce, shrubs and lichens. Only a small portion of the forests were logged and taken to a part-time sawmill at Watson Lake. Wonderful gardens are grown as far north as Dawson City.

Flying west some 60 miles near Almost Lake, I occasionally saw small herds of mountain caribou. Polar bears are found along the Beaufort Sea. Black and grizzly bear, timber wolves – including the tundra sub-species found north of the Porcupine River – and the large Alaska wolf are found all over the Yukon, being especially common in the west. Mule deer are found in the southern portion, and moose are plentiful in the interior. Farther north are small groups of woodland caribou. White Dall sheep are found in the north and southwest, and the dark brown stone sheep are located south of the Pelly River. Fannin sheep are also found here; they are white with dark saddles. All three species intermingle.

Birds of prey, such as peregrine falcons, bald and golden eagles, hawks and owls nest here, as do ducks, geese and trumpeter swans. Ptarmigan are one of the few birds that stay north all year long.

Pacific salmon spawn in rivers such as the Yukon tributaries. Trout, whitefish, pike and arctic grayling abound. Off the coast beluga (white whales), bowhead whales and bearded seals can be found. The Yukon is a fascinating place, and as the flying season began I was glad to be here once again.

May 16 I loaded our Super Cub with groceries and then fueled it. Hopping into the front seat of the Super Cub, I was soon strapped down. The dependable 150-horsepower Lycoming engine started quickly and sounded smooth. As I taxied to the Watson Lake runway I was really excited; this was my first trip of the season and after all the sanding and painting of the floats, I just wanted to fly and get away to some new adventure.

The flight was into the Shesly Strip, located southeast of the Asbestes town of Cassiar. Being airborne once again for the two-hour trip was refreshing, even if it was in a somewhat cramped airplane. After a circle over the outfitter's camp, I made my final approach at 65 mph for a normal three-point landing. The outfitter, Fletcher Day, a handsome, tall Tahltan Indian, wanted me to fly him to Cassier, which I did. Then I returned to Watson Lake, logging a total of 3.7 hours for the day.

In March Watson Lake Flying Service purchased the Beaver CF-FLN, which I flew most of the summer. Every Beaver had its own personality, and this one was not a favorite of mine. It didn't perform as well as my favorite red Beaver IBP, but maybe I was spoiled.

May 18 started a new adventure for me and IBP, as I would be flying it on wheel skis for the first time into Summit Lake, about 160 miles north. The lake was just inside the Yukon border, a few miles west of the Northwest Territories border. Cannex Mining and Exploration Company had chartered us to fly in supplies for a camp they were operating there. The lake was frozen, so they needed a ski-equipped airplane to bring in the supplies.

The wheel ski configuration on a beaver is operated by means of a hydraulic control unit located on the cockpit floor to the right of the pilot's seat. To lower the skis, you put the selection lever to the down position, which releases the hydraulic pressure and allows the pneumatic pressure in the upper portion of the activator housing to return the skis to the down position. To raise the skis you select up position and operate the hand pump until the skis are fully up, as shown by the needle on the indicator and, of course, visually check outside. Approximately 100 strokes of the hand pump are required to raise the skis fully. Your right arm gets a good workout, like doing curls with a barbell as the bicep gets pumped up. Because the skis trim safely in flight in any position, the pumping may be completed at the pilot's convenience. After getting airborne, the ski position has very little effect on air speed, flight characteristics, or center of gravity and can be left in up or down position as needed upon arrival at the landing field.

After loading the Beaver with groceries and camp gear, I cranked her up. Soon the reassuring roar of the Radial engine drowned out all other sounds. Applying full power and forward pressure on the elevator control, the tail wheel ski lifted and the Beaver flew off the runway at 60 mph in a slight tail down attitude. After reducing the throttle to 30 inches and the prop to 2,000 rpm, climb flap was selected and 95 mph (best rate of climb speed) was used until we reached our cruising altitude of 7500 feet. I followed Frances River on a northerly heading to the east arm of Frances Lake and then over Tillis Lake and McPherson Lake. Another 30 miles and I see the camp up on the south shore of Summit Lake.

Circling the camp area, I picked out where I would land. I began a descending turn to the left, flaps to land position, skis down and made the final approach at 80 mph. Depth perception was good, and I could see the snow and some tracks clearly in the bright sunshine. On a gray day, unbroken snow is like glassy water, and depth perception can be poor. Today's landing was smooth in the soft snow.

After unloading the supplies, I was soon airborne for Watson Lake. I logged in 2.9 hours for the trip. I had several trips scheduled the next day to Summit Lake – trips that were good moneymakers. I was paid mileage in addition to a very generous base salary from Watson Lake Flying Service.

Max Sanderson, a good friend of Jim and Stan, flew a helicopter for Cannex and would be flying out of this camp for the season. Max was in his fifties, a really interesting character who kept us all in stitches with his stories and one-liners. A gruff, no-nonsense kind of guy with a heart of gold, Max used to fly a Beaver for Cannex but he switched over to helicopters recently. He took me on my first helicopter ride here at Summit Lake. When we stopped forward speed in the air, I almost expected a stall, but it was a unique experience. Max had a smooth touch that made me feel comfortable. Max shared my low opinion of a de Havilland Otter DHC3, which carried double the payload of a Beaver His description of a good Otter pilot was someone four feet tall, four feet wide with a small hat size. In an Otter you spend much of your time bent over, loading heavy, cumbersome freight within the confines of the five-foot ceiling.

After a supply run to Summit Lake I headed back to the base.

Something I've always wanted to do but didn't want to try in case I screwed up was to loop and roll a Beaver. I was flying near Frances Lake at about 7,000 feet. I had recently finished an aerobatic course and decided to give IBP a bit of a workout. Diving to pick up speed, the Beaver seemed eager, and we did a couple good loops. Another slight dive to pick up speed, and I rolled IBP and held it inverted for a few seconds before completing the last half of the roll. A pleasant surprise – they had been hauling hay all winter! Now I had hay and dirt coming out of the cracks and crannies from the floor, settling on the panel, seats, windowsills and other places it shouldn't be. I certainly didn't want Jim and Stan to figure out what I'd been doing, so I spent some time brushing the hay and dirt back onto the floor. The Beaver performed like a champ and went through the loops and rolls like a pro. A few days later I told Jim Close what I did, and he just laughed. He had looped a Beaver on several occasion, he said.

The Beaver flies like a big Super Cub and is an excellent STOL (short takeoff and landing) airplane; however, you can't expect to crank it around like a Cub. Many Beavers have been stalled in a steep turn at a slow airspeed, often shortly after takeoff. It's a large airplane, requires a larger radius to turn, stalls at a higher airspeed than a Cub and has to be flown accordingly. So often too much is asked of any bush plane. There are limits, as wreckages strewn across the northern wilderness bear witness!

At the end of a rather long day, having made three trips into Summit, I logged 8.1 hours. Usually you can figure 8 flight hours requires about 16 hours of loading, unloading, servicing the airplane and waiting for people.

May 25 I logged 4.9 hours in the C-185 on floats; I flew into the Turnagain River and also made some side trips. My next trip was June 3 flying the Cessna 185 CF-YIG into Burnt Rose Lake and June Lake, logging a total of seven hours. The 185 was faster than the Beaver, indicating about 130-135 mph, but it doesn't perform as well or haul nearly the payload. It's quieter than the Beaver and was fun to fly occasionally.

Jim and Lois Close graciously let me stay at their home in Downtown Watson Lake for the summer. They had moved out to their lake cabin, which was close to the Seaplane Base. Scott joined me at the end of the school year in June. It was really great to have my son with me once again. I took Scott with me flying as often as I could. He thoroughly enjoyed co-piloting with Dad. He was a big help, pumping the floats, cleaning out the Beaver and helping to load. He was 13 years old, strong, well built and easy to get along with.

On June 11 I prepared our other Beaver CF-FLN for a trip into Almost Lake. Almost Lake was just that, more like a large pond. With care and a good airplane like the Beaver, we could operate out of it safely for the summer months. Hudson Bay Mining Company had decided to operate out of Almost Lake for the summer. The lake is about 90 miles west of Watson Lake in the Yukon Territory. The company would be prospecting this general area for the summer season.

I flew the tents, camp gear and food in first, along with several men, to get things going as rapidly as possible in this land of short seasons. By the end of the day I had made several trips, and camp was set up. I saw a small herd of caribou south of Almost Lake on a grass knoll, several moose at one end of Meister Lake, and a few more on some other lakes, wading in knee-deep water. The rest of the season I would be flying in men, food, mail, horse feed, etc., and flying out core samples. They had decided to use horses instead of a helicopter to keep costs down. Later they would see which was the most cost-effective mode of transportation for getting the job done.

Mining companies were a substantial part of our business some seasons. They took up the slack until the hunting seasons started, when we began taking hunters into the various outfitters' camps, shuttling that lasted until October or so.

June 24 I prepared our Beech 18 CF-NCL (a low wing medium twin engine airplane on floats) on a local checkout flight for myself. After fueling up, Jim Thibaudeau, our chief pilot and the one who flew the Beech most of the time, climbed in with me. I sat in the left hand pilot's seat with Jim in the co-pilot's seat.

The Beech had two Pratt & Whitney R-985 engines (the same engine that the Beaver uses). It was fun to fly a twin, especially with NCL on floats.

After pushing away from the dock I started first one engine, then the other and taxied to the south end of the lake. Run-up took a little longer, as I now had two engines to check. Everything was normal, and I applied full power. The Beech responded quickly because of the light load. With the 900 horses roaring, we left the water quickly. One hour of air work and landing, and we were back at the dock.

Most seaplanes won't get on the step if they're heavily loaded and conditions are bad. The beech 18 gets on the step quickly and will get in the air under adverse conditions and heavy loads, but because of the thin high-speed wing it sometimes doesn't want to climb. Occasionally on hot days the engines start to overheat, and you might have to go 100 miles to gain 1,000 feet. As soon as you get airborne, the plane vibrates, indicating it is close to a stall! The Beaver with a thick high-lift wing climbs much faster and is a much better bush plane. I told one of the owners of the company that I felt that the Beech 18 was going to kill some pilot! After I made a few flights, I refused to fly it anymore.

On June 26 I flew NCL into Quartz Lake several times on a freight haul for a mining camp with Jim sitting in the right-hand seat. Although the Beech was an interesting machine to fly, I decided the Beaver was my favorite, and I preferred it over all others.

Near the end of June I loaded the Beaver FLN with supplies for Hudson Bay Mining Company to be taken into Almost and Erwin lakes, which are in the same area. Scott helped with the loading. He was going to stay in the camp at Almost Lake for a few days to do some fishing. Scott, like most boys at 13, loved to put away the grub. The camp had excellent chow; steaks and roast were normal daily fare, with potatoes, gravy and freshly made pie

Scott climbed aboard the Beaver and sat in the co-pilot seat while I pushed off the dock and climbed into the pilot's seat. Climbing over the lake with a gentle turn to the left, I flew a westerly heading to put us on course to Almost Lake. I let Scott have the controls, as I often did; he was a good co-pilot and enjoyed flying.

The country was fairly flat for about 40 miles before we began flying through the Cassiar Mountains with several peaks at nearly 7,000 feet. We were following the Little Moose River and were lower than the peaks. After flying over a pass at the headwater of the Moose River, we picked up Irvin Creek and could see Irvin Lake sparkling in the distance. We caught a glimpse of some moose near the lake in a meadow. We landed, unloaded supplies and departed for Almost Lake a few miles away.

Almost Lake came into view as we flew over a mountain range. I checked the wind on the lake surface and saw it was from the southwest. We made a descending turn over the north side of the lake and approached into the wind, touching down close to the northeastern shore. The lake was small, and I did not want to overshoot. Once the floats touched, I brought power back to idle. We slowed down rapidly, settling into the water like a heavy duck.

Men came from camp as we taxied toward shore. We tied the Beaver and made a human chain to unload the supplies. Mostly the men were interested in the mail, something eagerly sought in isolated camps.

The cook's tent had a plywood floor and wood stove. We enjoyed coffee and some home-cooked rolls. Scott met Dan, the cook, and the other men who would be his mates at this camp for the next several days. His likable nature soon made him fit into his temporary home.

After coffee and a good conversation, I slowly walked down to the white Beaver CF-FLN. I breathed the fresh air, viewed this remote valley and the mountains above and was thankful for my flying job and the opportunity to see this vast country and to play my many roles as a pilot.

The other ways I've made a living pale in comparison to this unique job. This is partly because flying is a respectable, necessary and rewarding career, but mostly for me it is because flying had been such a love of mine since my youth.

The fascination of actually piloting an airplane, the takeoff, flying through the mountains and landing in these wilderness lakes was a breath-taking experience. Big troubles in life shrink into proper perspective. The changing conditions of weather and country, the challenge of increasing my knowledge and skill of piloting and the satisfaction of a job well done all contributed to a fulfilling means of making a living and of satisfying my inner man. I especially enjoyed sharing the north country with my clients. Not all flights were smooth; sometimes passengers and pilot got grey hairs. Winds, short and treacherous strips, lakes, river landings, bad weather and pilot fatigue can contribute to an uncomfortable ride. But by the next day, the discomfort is only a memory, and I'm ready to crank up the Beaver for another adventure. One thing I've noticed: if a smooth landing can be pulled off, people usually consider it a good flight, maybe because it was the last thing they remember. So I always try to make a good approach and gentle touchdown, although I don't always succeed.

The trip back to Watson Lake from Almost Lake was a pleasant flight. I logged 3.9 hours for the day. It was June 29 when Jim Close informed me, "Larry, you have a flight to Godlin Lakes in the Northwest Territory. Then you will fly up to Norman Wells to pick up more supplies and return to Godlin." An outfitter had chartered the Beaver. It would be a moneymaker for me, with interesting company and an interesting trip into a new area. It was 255 miles one way into Godlin Lakes and another 125 miles from there to Norman Wells, close to 800 miles total!

Godlin Lakes consists of three lakes near the headwaters of the Godlin River in a valley that runs north and south. The lakes are due north of Watson, and I calculated the flying time at just around two hours. Once again I'd be flying into the rugged MacKenzie Mountains. The course would parallel the Hyland River, cross the South Nahanni River, over O'Grady Lake, June Lake and over the Elwi River. Just a few miles north of there lay my destination – Godwin Lakes.

After fueling up and doing my walk around I put some extra fuel in. I would be able to fuel up at Norman Wells; there was an oil refinery there. Norman Wells gas was considerably cheaper than at Watson

Lake, but I might need extra fuel. It was always wise to leave some extra ten-gallon cans at this camp as a reserve for later trips. The Beaver carried about three hours of fuel and the reserve, so we often had to carry extra gas on longer trips.

The flight up was smooth as I climbed to 8,000 feet and had a wonderful view of the country. I landed in the middle lake, unloaded the supplies and then headed for Norman Wells. There groceries and camp gear were quickly loaded and I was soon heading back to Godlin Lakes. After unloading again at the middle lake, I had a quick coffee break and headed back to home base.

July 2nd I flew into Tootsi Lake, about 60 miles southwest of Watson Lake. The trip was uneventful except for the gusty conditions on the lake surface. One nice thing about flying into a lake is that by reading the marks it makes on the water surface, you can tell if the wind is gusty, if it's coming from several different directions, or if it changes direction part way down. Surface gusts caused a hairy landing approach and an up-and-down ride, but we finally landed, taxied to shore and unloaded gear and supplies for prospectors.

A couple days later I flew into Daughney and Erwin Lake for Hudson Bay Mining Company, then picked up Scott at Almost Lake. Scott had caught some nice trout, eaten a lot better food than he got at home and had made some new friends.

On July 21st I flew my favorite Beaver IBP into Swan Lake, 90 miles from Watson Lake. I was flying for Mr. MacCaully who had a guiding territory in his area. He was someone for whom I would do a lot of flying later in the season. Swan Lake adjoins the Alaska Highway on its northern shore. MacCaully guided moose hunts close by, as well as trips for other game, such as caribou, sheep and bear at other lakes near here, lakes accessible only by float plane or horseback. After a few more flights for other outfitters, July was history.

August started out fairly busy. We flew mail and supplies into various outfitters' camps, since the hunting season was underway. The most sought-after trophy was the stone sheep. Frank Cooke seemed to have one of the best areas, both in number of sheep taken and also for size, although I had noticed in all the areas the size of the horns seemed to decrease over the past several years, partly due to the heavy hunting pressure, I thought.

After work one night and before bed Scott said, "Dad, what do you think about buying a taildragger?" "Well, son, maybe a Super Cub someday or a Citabria would be a fun airplane," I replied. Scott was an avid airplane buff, and our conversation usually got around to flying.

The alarm went of at 5:00 a.m. I had a 6:00 a.m. flight in the Beaver. After a nourishing "stick to your ribs" breakfast of oatmeal, we jumped into the Volvo and drove to the seaplane base.

After gassing the plane and checking the oil, I did a visual inspection of the airplane, checking to see if the elevators and ailerons were working properly, looking at the float fittings, nuts, bolts, cables and checking the prop for nicks. When taxiing downwind, the water often causes nicks, which we file down from time to time Sometimes I took the round blade of a screwdriver and ran it over the nicks to smooth the prop down a bit. Care in taxiing was essential to keep the nicks to a minimum. We flew to Frank Cooke's camp at Scoop Lake.

One day while doing a pre-flight inspection of the Beaver I noticed a thick bolt that connected the float to the airframe had a loose nut, and if it came off it could have caused a fatal accident. It's so important to check your plane over carefully before flying!

We overnighted at Scoop Lake and after sundown went skinny-dipping in the lake. We were sweaty, and it was very smoky because of many forest fires. After the sunset I said, "Scott, look at the setting sun and remember it in later years. See the old log cabin and the pole-covered fence and the lake in the background." We still talk about that from time to time, sharing our memories of that special place and time.

After a short sleep in a tent on the sandy beach of Scoop Lake we left at about 5:00 a.m. and flew to Colt Lake, a tiny lake high in the mountains 20 miles southwest of here. We had groceries and camp supplies to freight in and were kept busy flying, loading and unloading for several hours before returning to Watson Lake.

One day near Bluesheep Lake I flew low over a peak and started down the other side, which was fairly open. A large grizzly stood on his hind legs, angry at my invasion of his space and swatted at the Beaver as though it were a pesky fly.

I logged the most hours I've ever flown in a single day on August 10. After trips up to the South Nahanni in the Northwest Territories and trips down to Moodie Lake and other lakes for Frank Cooke, I had put in 12.8 hours of flying time. I was flying lots of long days – total hours for the month of August 1973 were 193 hours, probably the most I've ever flown in a single month. About half of that was double mileage, as anything over 10,000 miles in a single month pays double. It was an exhausting month.

To pick up some geologists I made a trip into a small river east of Watson Lake that runs into the Liard River. Landing on the Liard I taxied up the small river, heading north. It was clear and looked about five feet deep. About a half mile upstream I saw the men on the east bank of the river.

The water was very swift and clear as I nudged up to the bank, holding the front right float to the bank, and I had to leave the engine running with lots of power. The men jumped aboard; a couple crawled in the back door and sat down. One man who had a bad foot climbed up in the co-pilot's seat and caught the door with his bad foot. The door flipped off the hinge and sank to the bottom of the raging river.

I taxied out from shore and turned downstream toward the Liard. Once I reached the Liard I headed upstream, trying to locate the door. Sure enough, we could see it coming downstream, bouncing on the bottom. A couple of the men tried to catch it and almost fell in. I yelled, "Forget it!" it was gone. "Let's get out of here before someone falls in." My nervous passenger sitting next to the doorless opening in the side of the Beaver leaned toward me all the way back to Watson Lake as the wind whistled around him. Back at Watson Lake, Wally fixed a makeshift solid plywood door cover. I flew the plane that way until a replacement arrived.

On September 21st I flew into a lake for Murd MacCaully, the outfitter. My destination was Goodwin Lake about 130 miles southwest of Watson Lake in northern B.C. and just a few miles west of the south end of Teslin Lake.

I had some hunters going in and some coming out. After about an hour of flight we flew over the camp, which was on the east shore. The lake runs north and south. Sure enough, I could see the wind from four different directions (on the water) and a wind shear about where the camp was. The wind went north and south from that point. I saw severe gusts all over the lake, which looked like someone had thrown splotches of ink on the surface.

"Hang on!" I told my passengers as I made another hairy approach. I made my approach faster than normal to compensate for the gusts, wind shear and crosswinds. I wanted a little extra air speed for a cushion. Until the Beaver was on the water and off the step, anything could happen and often did. That knowledge kept me alert, my knuckles white and my body a bit tense. This was one of those lakes I would rather not fly to, money or no money, but it was part of my job and had to be done.

As I neared the surface, the Beaver began a fight with an unseen floe. First up, then down, the wind blew us sideways to the left, then the right and hammered us relentlessly in all directions.

Finally there seemed to be a bit of a let-up, and I touched down. "Ah, we're home free!" I thought. But a gust picked us up again. We had to make a couple more touchdowns before I could pull the power and settle into the water. It was nice to be safely on the water, although we were still being buffeted with gusts.

Taxiing to the camp, I shut FLN down and glided into a makeshift pole dock. I needed a cup of coffee to settle my nerves and a few minutes on firm ground before I was ready to think of leaving.

After loading up the returning hunters with their sheep trophies and gear, we taxied out to the west end. We had a tail wind as I began that takeoff run. The Beaver got on the step okay, but as we reached flying speed the wind started to do crazy things. It hit us from many different directions. I wanted an excess of speed on the step before I flew off, because I was sure we would hit one or more wind shears, and I didn't want to be dumped hard back into the lake. Finally I pulled it off with excess airspeed, holding the plane close to the water until a safe airspeed was reached. Then I began a gentle climb. We were buffeted from many directions, and I was busy trying to keep the Beaver in the air to gain some altitude. Soon the north end of the lake slipped below, and I turned to the east, down a valley toward Teslin Lake and some smooth air, I hoped. As I crossed Teslin Lake the air was smoother, and I could relax, watching the country slip by. I still dislike that lake with a passion.

Scott caught a flight on CPA to Prince George and returned to school once again. He had a few stories to tell his mom and his schoolmates. It was always a sad time as we said our goodbyes. However, I would see my son next month when the flying season was over.

Jack O'Conner, who was the outdoor editor for *Outdoor Life*, was a renowned hunter who hunted over most of the world, including Africa for lions and other game. He was an expert on rifles and ballistics. He came to Watson Lake to hunt, and on two occasions I flew him out to different camps. I flew him into Colt Lake in the early 1970s, and he shot a nice stone sheep, which was his last ram.

Jack, who was in his seventies then and reminded me a great deal of my grandfather, lived in Lewiston, Idaho. It was very interesting for me to sit and listen to his stories about his hunts and to discuss rifles while we were in Frank Cooke's camp. He was a bit of a white-knuckle flier, and the weather wasn't very good when I flew him to Colt Lake. There was rain, fog and low clouds, but it was flyable, although we had to do some dodging through low clouds in order to arrive at Colt Lake. Jack was glad to get his feet back on solid ground.

Later I corresponded with Jack. He died a few years ago. I had read Jack's stories from the time I was a boy and felt privileged to have met him and to fly this man who was a legend in the hunting fraternity. The guide on that last sheep hunt said Jack was still an excellent shot. A picture of Jack O'Conner, me and another hunter on the trip to Colt Lake hangs on my office wall.

At an earlier date in the late '60s Jack O'Conner and his wife came to Smithers, B.C., and one of my fellow pilots at Omineca Air Service flew them out to a camp where they went on a trail ride into a wilderness area of northern British Columbia with an outfitter for a week or so.

Jack shot a stone sheep on each of the two hunts I flew him on. Colt Lake is a puddle at about 4,000 feet in elevation, dammed up on the west end by a beaver dam. There is a cache on stilts at the northeast end of the lake, and we had to be careful when landing or taking off in that direction so we didn't hit it. The tent camp was located near the cache. Colt Lake was ideal, since at 4,000 feet the hunters didn't have to climb much higher to be in the middle of excellent stone sheep country, probably the best area of North America for this species.

At this time there wasn't any limit on the number of sheep that could be taken out of a guide's area. Now each guiding area has only a limited number of permits issued for each season by the Game Department.

One late evening in September just before dark I managed to fly into Colt Lake to spend the night. I knew there were some young ladies in camp who were excellent cooks. Frank's camps were known for their good food, and I always tried to fly in, if possible, around dinner time, so it was no accident that I lighted here on this particular evening. I had been flying for Gary Moore, near Skook's old ranch south of here.

After a good feed the boys, Frank Jr. And some other guides started to tell what I thought were tall tales. They spoke of flying saucers and swore they visited the camp after dark, flying nearby. I listened tongue-in-cheek, trying not to laugh and told them, "Oh sure, what else is new?" As it got dark, the stars stood out sharply in the clean mountain air, and sure enough, up high overhead, I could see moving objects, which I was sure were satellites. But in a short time, a pinpoint of light many miles east of the Kechika River and beyond the distant Rocky Mountains appeared. Within a few seconds the light became a rather large pulsating object, hovering over the Kechika River. It must have gone 50 miles in a couple seconds. The hunters in camp were looking through a spotting scope on a stand, which I also used, and we saw a pulsating light beam emitted from this stationary object hovering maybe a mile high and seven miles away. It soon disappeared in a few seconds to the east over the Rocky Mountains, then a little later reappeared the same way, at the same terrific speed! I was stone sober and have no explanation for what we saw. It was a strange experience – unreal – but I was there and experienced this happening.

One day after landing at Moodie Lake, which at the time was Frank Cooke's main headquarters, I was instructed by Frank to fly a young lady by the name of Dee Dee and her baby to another camp of Frank's. Dee Dee was a cook and a relative of Frank's. I applied full power and, after getting on the step in the Beaver, the oil cap, which is visible and below the panel, came off and hot oil sprayed all over us. I immediately shut the engine off, and we came to a quick stop, dead in the water.

Frank couldn't figure out what was going on and came out in the boat to see what the problem was. He then helped us clean up the mess. After putting more oil in and securing the cap, I again applied full power, and we were soon in the air, this time making a safe flight to Frank's camp at Colt Lake.

A unique phenomenon happens during the fall. The northern lights are at times spectacular. Sometimes it's like you're in a round room, and they are all about; other times it's like a moving curtain on a stage, with the curtain waving, changing form and color. It adds mystery to the North and is one of the special events that became part of my life.

One afternoon when I was in Scoop Lake on a charter for Frank, I took a short flight just south of the lake and counted about 300 moose. It was like a large cattle ranch. There is a lot of marsh and feed here for the moose, and horses can be wintered here as well, living off the land, as the grass is abundant and the winters are relatively mild. Frank and Skook left their horses here over the winter months.

The outfitters have been known to start fires here. After the ground is burned, the new growth makes excellent moose feed. The forest service frowns a bit on this practice, but it was carried out successfully and, as far as I know, they never caught anyone. But I am sure they knew who the fire bugs were.

The many flights for Frank and his sons will always remain as some of my most cherished and memorable times in the North, as I flew over some of the most beautiful wilderness areas in North America with the magnificent, rugged Rocky Mountains (my favorite mountains) visible just a few miles to the east. I also had the best fishing in my life at Denetiah Lake. Denetiah Lake is in Frank's hunting area. I heard George Dalziel planted those Rainbow trout years ago, as he did in numerous other lakes in this country.

Jim Close's accountant had purchased an Aztec, which was a piper twin-engine wheel plane. He was going to lease it back to Watson Lake Flying Service. Because I was the only one in the company to have flown an Aztec (the one in Seattle that I used to obtain my ATP), I was elected to pick it up in Calgary, Alberta.

I caught a connecting flight to Calgary and did a circuit at the airport with a pilot before departing for Dawson Creek. The flight from Calgary to Dawson took 2.7 hours flying time.

This plane performed exceptionally well. The normal 260-horsepower engines had been replaced with 290-horsepower fuel-injected Lycoming engines, and it made a real performer out of it. After flying at 120 in the Beaver all summer, it was nice to cruise along at about 200, and it was fun to have two engines to play with! It kept me on my toes, and it was just a lot more interesting. The seats were cushy, like a comfortable reclining armchair. After fueling up at Dawson Creek, the next leg took me to Fort Nelson, where I landed and fueled up again before the final leg to Watson Lake.

I made my first trip on October 11 in our new Aztec CF-HIA with paying customers. I flew them into Fort Liard, in the Northwest Territories, 190 miles one way. The trip was smooth and took only about one hour flying time. After refueling, I tried to start the engines. However, when they're hot and you try to restart them, sometimes they get a vapor lock, and then I would let them set for a time. These fuel-injected engines were much more temperamental than an engine with a carburetor. After letting them cool down, I once again hit the starter and got first one engine started and then the other one. After a while I learned the necessary tricks to starting these engines and had few problems after that.

The trip back was pleasant, as the air was fairly smooth, and I was beginning to feel more comfortable flying a twin again. It was a nice change, however, the Beaver was still my favorite. This was like a sports car, a fun airplane to fly, but the Beaver was still the workhorse of the North, as far as I was concerned.

The next day Frank Cooke booked the Aztec HIA to fly into Scoop Lake where he now had a landing strip and several new cabins for hunters. One building had toilets and showers and was a big change from the old days of an outhouse and a washbasin. However, this was only at the main camp. Once the hunters left here, it was horseback and walking and using the Johnson bar or a trip behind a bush to take care of nature's call.

At 200 mph, the trips to HIA were noticeably shorter. Over the next few days I flew into Dease Lake, Skook's ranch at Terminus Mountain, and Frank's camp at Scoop Lake. My last flight of 1973 was in the Beaver FLN. I flew to Teslin, Burnt Rose Lake, which was just north of the Turnagain River, then back to Watson Lake, logging 4.0 hours.

Jim Close certified my logbook from May 16, 1973 through October 20, 1973 for a total of 638.4 hours, the most I've flown in a season. This was also the longest season I'd flown in the Yukon. The days had been long, time off almost non-existent. Fortunately there had been no accidents, although there were some close calls, a few grey hairs started and maybe a few hairs lost. But it had been a good season, I had new adventures, flew some new airplanes and had an enjoyable time for the most part. Attending the Annual Fireman's Ball, I had a great time celebrating with most of the town.

October 21, 1973 – Last day for Watson Flying Service, I wrote in the journal I started a few years ago, "No accidents. Feel worn out!"

Larry Snaig at his fishing camp on Tobally Lakes in the Yukon where he guided fishermen and trapped. He has a unique log cabin on the lake that he traps out of and guides fishermen. He is a happy good natured man that loves the wilderness.

Larry taxied up a small river off the Laird River to pick up some geologist. One of the men who had a club foot caught the edge of the door and it fell into the river and we lost it. It was one windy Beaver flying home... Wally made a plywood door until we could order another Beaver door.

Chapter 8

HOWARD'S PASS | WHITE KNUCKLE STRIP

Today was the day to head north for another flying season at Watson Lake, April 20, 1974. I climbed into my reliable 1972 blue Volvo, departing the Seattle area on course for Watson Lake via the Alaskan Highway. It took three days of driving to reach Watson Lake.

For the next several days I hibernated in my home on the shore of Watson Lake. I had bought a trailer the year before and had it on my lake lot, just across the bay from Watson Lake Flying Service seaplane base. Sometimes I canoed to work. It was nice to be alone to collect my thoughts, review the past winter and plot a course for my future.

Last December my son Scott and I drove to Spokane for the Christmas holidays with my parents and relatives, having a good, warm visit with all. In Seattle, Scott picked up some bamboo poles to use in the construction of a hang glider that he intended to build. Fortunately he decided not to proceed, much to my relief. We toured the underground city that lies beneath the present city of Seattle and had a wonderful time.

On March 23rd I had departed Seattle for Hawaii to visit a high school buddy, Gary Johnson. We joined the naval reserves together while in high school. Gary made a career out of the Navy and was now a Lieutenant J.G. stationed at Pearl Harbor. Gary met me at the airport, and I stayed the first night with him and then stayed at the Coco Palms for $10 a night. It was about one block from the beach and had a kitchen, so I was able to fix some of my meals there. I flew to Maui the next day for a couple days there. The trip to Hawaii, which lasted a week, was a relaxing time. It was good to see my old high school buddy again. It was nice to relax in the sun and body surf. When Gary and I were in Honolulu in the mid '50s it was a quiet, sleepy town with very few buildings over a couple stories. Now it looked like a big eastern city with many tall buildings and packed with people.

But it was great to be back to the land I loved on my own place – which was now paid for – and to enjoy the freedom of spirit that I felt in this great land called the Yukon. Again I was spending my days working in the hangar, repairing floats and sanding and painting so all would be ready when the float season got underway. The Master Painter touched the quaking Aspen along the lake with a light green, and seemingly overnight the meadows came alive with new growth; spring was upon us here in the Yukon. A glorious time, a new season had begun.

I had my first flight of the season in my favorite Beaver CF-IBP on May 28 and made a short local flight. It was really great to be back in the air and flying over the country I loved. May 29th I had my first flight booked to Howard's Pass in IBP on wheel skis, for Hudson Bay Mining Company. Russ MacIntosh was in charge of the camp located in the mountains just a few miles north of Summit Lake, 160 air miles from Watson Lake, close to the Northwest Territories border. There were still several feet of snow at this camp. This was an exploration camp, and a lot of drilling had been done. Because the core samples looked good, there was a good chance the site would become a mine.

The Beaver was loaded with a lot of canned goods, some staples and various mining equipment. Climbing into IBP brought back many memories, most of adventures on floats. Now flying wheel skis would create new ones.

Taxiing to the end of the paved strip at the Watson Lake airport, which was run by the Department of Transportation, I did a run-up, then called air radio and let them know I was ready for departure and checked to see if any airplanes were in the area. "None reported," he said. I acknowledged and stated that I was departing for Howard's Pass, filed a flight note with him and then lined up with the center of the runway. Full power was applied, the skis were up and I was using the wheels since the snow was gone at the airport.

The air was cool, and the Beaver responded quickly. In a slight tail down attitude I let the Beaver fly off at about 60 mph and then reduced the throttle to 30 inches (mp), the prop to 2000 rpm and pumped up the flaps to the climb position. We were indicating 95 mph – our best rate of climb speed.

Once I reached an altitude of about 7,000 feet I pumped the flaps up and reduced the throttle to 28 inches of manifold pressure and the prop to 1800 rpm. The airspeed indicated about 120 mph. As soon as the engine had time to cool a bit, I leaned the mixture setting until the engine lost a little power, then enriched the mixture a bit until the engine smoothed out. I set my trim and enjoyed the scenery, which was mostly dark forest, blanketed on the ground by snow.

The reliability of this engine was comforting to me, as I had never had a Beaver engine quit yet; I trusted it with my life. On many occasions, an engine failure on takeoff would probably buy me the farm.

The Beaver engine was changed every 1,000 hours, and a rebuilt R985 was put in. This was a mandatory regulation from the Canadian Department of Transportation for Canadian planes. In Alaska, planes are not restricted to the 1,000 hours but can fly much longer. After flying on the Alaska coast in an engine that was clapped out, I really appreciated the strict Canadian regulations. In some cases, such as during bad fire seasons when the plane was needed urgently, the Department of Transportation would give a 100-hour extension if the compression check was okay.

Flying north along the Frances River I wondered what the snow condition would be this late in the season. The airstrip was at about 4700 feet; the snow trip was about 1500 feet long, which didn't leave a lot of room with the high altitude. Even with the supercharged engine, the performance would be considerably less than at Watson Lake.

Frances Lake appeared below and soon slipped behind – about 60 miles to go. Summit Lake was now visible. As I flew up a valley northeast of Summit Lake, the camp came into view. As I circled the camp I took a good look and noticed the strip with an altitude of about 5,000 feet ran east and west. I made the final approach toward the east at about 80 mph with landing flaps. As I got near the snow strip I slowed down to about 70 mph and rounded out, touching down about 100 feet from the end of the strip. The snow was soft and granulated; it slowed the Beaver rapidly. I used power to get to the other end of the strip where there was lots of help to unload. Then the help and I headed to the cook tent for coffee.

The large cook tent was at the eastern end of the camp and on the north side of the strip. Near the cook tent was a radio shack with wire antennas strung to nearby trees and posts. The rest of the camp lay toward the west. Each tent had a plywood floor and a stove inside and would accommodate four bunks comfortably. Just above the camp on a mountain pass there was a rough airstrip built with a dogleg in the middle. After the sun melted the snow strip, I would fly the Beaver on wheels into this strip. Near the far west end of camp was a diesel generator that supplied electric power to the camp.

After about 20 minutes of good conversation, strong coffee and fresh baked pastries, I headed back to the Beaver with some outgoing mail and a couple of passengers. Because the snow was soft, it took a little while before we picked up much speed. About three-fourths of the way down the strip we finally lifted off. I had wondered if I would run off the strip before getting airborne. The trip went well, but I could see the strip was deteriorating rapidly, and it wouldn't be long before the ski season ended at Howard's Pass. I made almost daily flights from Watson Lake into Howard's Pass until June 14, which was the last trip I felt could be made safely. The snow strip had broken up badly; the Beaver broke through in several places, and I almost got stuck.

In my journal I wrote the following: "This was a grey hair run as the snow strip was breaking up. Getting off this short strip of 1500 feet at 5,000 feet elevation was a nervous proposition – especially when hauling equipment and men!" I logged 62.1 hours on wheel skis into Howard's Pass from May 29 to June 14 – not bad, since June was usually a slow period.

June 18 I purchased Scott's ticket on CPA from Prince George to Watson Lake and talked to the foreman at the local sawmill, hoping to get employment for Scott there. He said there were no openings at present.

I had been continuing my running program, and on the evening of June 21 I ran three miles. Running gave me a real high, and I had been doing it for five years. It helped keep my weight below 200 pounds most of the time. I was in good shape, as I also lifted an assortment of weights. I wrote in my journal, "This run was very invigorating; the fragrance of the flowers and greenery filled my lungs with sweetness. I felt like the wind and ran effortlessly!" At least that was what the journal said!

Scott arrived at the airport for the summer on June 24 and settled in at my lake place. After a good night's sleep, Scott and I headed for the seaplane base. I was getting a checkout on our Beech 18 CF-NCL from Jim Thibaudeau, our chief pilot. One and a half hours of circuits and bumps (landings) and some air work with Jim constituted my checkout. The following day I flew the Beech one-hour solo.

Gordon Scott, an apprentice engineer, hopped aboard with me in our Beaver IBP, and we flew into the Hudson Bay Mining Camp at Almost Lake. Gordon was an easy-going guy and did a good job for us doing checks and maintenance on the various planes.

It was now July, Independence Day in the U.S.A. but not up here, and Scott was doing some fishing. Scott and I headed to the Texaco service station in town where Scott landed his first job, at $3 an hour. I was really proud and felt confident he would do okay. The station fueled most of the trucks that came along the Alaska Highway, and Scott would be pumping lots of diesel, as well as changing flat truck tires weighing about 200 pounds. Scott was husky and strong for his 14 years.

July 7 I fueled the Beech 18 CF-NCL and loaded gear for a trip into Dal Lake, Northwest Territories, for Lori Bliss who had a guiding territory in that area. The flight into Dal Lake took about two hours, part of it over the rugged Mackenzie Mountains. The trip was without problems. This was my first real trip with the Beech on a freight haul, and I would be gone several days on a new adventure.

145

After landing at Dal Lake I flew over to Wrigley along the Mackenzie River in the Northwest Territories, about half way between Fort Simpson and Fort Norman. After landing I taxied to a dock and began loading freight in the Beech for the trip back to Dal Lake. To save money, Lori had horse feed and camping gear barged into Wrigley earlier. I would be making shuttle flights for a few days from here to Dal Lake.

It was getting late, so I decided to call it a day and overnight at Wrigley. It was a small community on the east bank of the mighty Mackenzie River. It was quiet and peaceful there, as if the clock had stopped years ago and time stood still. It didn't get dark at that time of year, but I finally managed to get to bed around midnight. I slept well, but morning came too quickly. After a bite to eat, I walked down to the river to ready the Beech for the day's first flight to Dal Lake.

As I tried to start the engines, I discovered the battery was dead. It took a few hours to remove and recharge the battery. After the delay, the 100-mile flight to Dal Lake took less than an hour. Several of Lori's guides helped me unload, and I was soon off to Wrigley for another load. By the end of the day I'd logged 5.7 flying hours. Because of the battery trouble it had been a long and frustrating day, considering the amount of time I had actually flown. Overnighting again at Wrigley I reviewed the day's events and felt some frustration with the Beech. Once again the Beaver, which was so trouble-free, stood head and shoulders above the Beech and the single engine Otter. I was spoiled!

The new day was clear and warm, with very little breeze here on the Mackenzie River. After breakfast I wandered down to the Beech and discovered the battery was dead. I had to have it charged once again. Frustration soon set in, and I felt jinxed. I wished I could trade this plane off for my reliable Beaver IBP, which I really missed now. One flight from Wrigley to Hook Lake and back was all I had time for because of the trouble with the battery.

July 9 I logged 5.6 hours on three round trips to Hook Lake. July 10 I made one trip to Hook Lake from Wrigley and then the welcome trip back to Watson Lake.

Howard's Pass was my destination on a hot 12th of July. I was taking the Beaver FLN on wheels into the strip. The muddy strip had about 1,000 usable feet. It lay on a 5500-foot pass with very tricky winds and had a dogleg curve in the middle, sloping into a draw on the east side.

The usual crosswind was coming down from the mountain from the west side of the north-south strip, blowing directly across the runway into the draw. Approaching from the south, the strip looked something like an aircraft carrier. The edge on the south side dropped about 60 degrees down, and I usually experienced a down draft. Today was no different; one quarter to a half mile out an invisible hand pushed me down below the level of the runway. I had to increase power substantially to get back on the proper approach altitude. As I got close to the end of the strip, I had to cut all power, because the down draft quit and I could overshoot.

Touchdown! Mud was flying through the prop and solidly filling my windscreen. Meanwhile I kept the left wing down with left aileron to compensate for the crosswind as I skidded around the left dogleg, trying to keep from getting sucked into the draw, something which would certainly have wrecked the airplane and probably ended my career.

The Beaver finally slid to a stop in the mud. Even sitting in the middle of a mud hole I felt relief at being safe. I unloaded and took off to the south, trying to get up enough speed in the mud to get airborne before going off the south end of the strip. That end dropped off at about a 60-degree slope. If I was not airborne, I would have a wild ride bouncing down the mountainside. Lucky Day! I was airborne about 100 feet before the drop-off. What a relief it was every time I made a successful landing and takeoff and flew back to Watson Lake in one piece!

This was probably the toughest, hairiest strip that I'd ever operated off, and every trip kept me on the edge. However, there was always the tremendous high after pulling out of any tight, risky situation. Living on the edge, with my life on the line, and getting away with it was hard to describe. It had its own reward and made me feel I'd done something worthwhile.

One of our pilots refused to fly into that strip anymore, because he once didn't get airborne by the time he passed the south end of the runway. He bounced down the mountainside before getting enough airspeed to fly. I heard the story from one of the Hudson Bay Mining Camp geologists at the airstrip. It just gave me something else to worry about, since I could easily visualize it happening, especially when the strip was muddy and it took so much longer to get up to flying speed.

One day I made an "aircraft carrier" landing, right on the end of the strip with a payload of canned food. I hit solidly – too solidly. The impact bent a bulkhead just in front of the tail wheel. The skin was wrinkled, but I was able to take off safely. After I made the hard landing, one of the mining men at the strip said, "Wow! That sure was a good landing; you put it down right on the end of the strip." His comment didn't make me feel superior as I viewed the damage to the aircraft. Later, landing on the long, wide, paved Watson Lake strip was pure joy. It took Jim Close one day to fix the wrinkle, having to replace some skin and beef up and straighten the bulkhead.

I wrote in my journal the next few days, "Have obtained a 26-foot Corsair trailer, self-contained, and have it on my property at the lake. Nice location, but we don't have water or electricity yet. The hungry mosquitoes waited outside the door to jump Scott and me when we had to do nature's bidding over a Johnson bar." I previously owned a smaller trailer on the property.

On July 21 I passed the 9,000-mile mark in flying for the month. After 10,000 miles I will get paid double mileage. I flew to Ross River twice, then to Howard's Pass and on to Cantung and returned to Watson Lake. My son's smiling face greeted me at the dock.

I wrapped up July with several more trips into Howard's Pass for Hudson Bay Mining Company, some flights into Irwin and Doughney Lake for the same company, a trip into Hook Lake and then a trip into Tuya Lake (Frank Stewart's hunting camp) and Netson Lake on the 31st.

August started out well; I logged 9.6 hours on the first, flying into Provinger and Scoop Lake with my favorite Beaver CF-IBP. I made two trips into Howard's Pass in the wheel Beaver FLN over the next couple of days, then made a trip into the Cadillac Strip just northwest of Deadman's Valley for a mining company. On August 6 I flew the red Beaver into Flat and Glacier Lake and to Summit Lake the next day.

It was a beautiful day August 8, as I taxied IBP out into Watson Lake. I had a trip into Provinger Lake, which was located about 130 miles south in northern B.C. Huge boulders of jade weighing several tons lie along this lake and in the surrounding areas, keeping several companies and individual prospectors busy working during the short summer months. Jade is extremely hard and had to be sawed with a diamond blade into 80-pound chunks that could be flown out in the Beaver. It was a slow process, but when they had a load ready, they gave us a call and we picked it up.

Larry Barr was overseeing the jade operation in Provinger Lake. Two brothers, Andy and Paul Jenson, were avid prospectors and had some good property on nearby lakes. They were in the process of striking an arrangement with some Chinese businessmen who wanted some of their jade for the commercial market. Jerry Davis, a good friend of Jim and Stan's and a super nice guy, had some good jade property in the area on Boulder Lake close to the Turnagain River. Jerry and his wife, two of the nicest people I met in the bush, spent the summer working their property. Jerry flew his own green Super Cub and was an excellent pilot. Another prospector close to Jerry from Mount Vernon, Washington, gave me a gold nugget in a plastic paperweight, which I keep on my desk.

I had propane, groceries and some mining gear, and of course the mail to fly in and would be flying some men and gear back to Watson Lake. After run-up and about a 40-second run on the lake, IBP flew off the water, gently climbed and turned to the left toward the south. I relaxed and continued the climb to 7,000 feet; it was a clear day, and I enjoyed the safety of altitude.

Flying over the Dease River and coming up to the west side of the Horse Ranch Range, I got a nice updraft. Soon Cry Lake took form, and we flew east of the north end, paralleling the Turnagain River for a few miles. Provinger Lake appeared. The camp was visible on the south end, and I circled as we descended to make the final approach to the south into the wind. After touching down I taxied on the step until we were a few hundred feet from shore, reducing power to idle in order to slip slowly into the makeshift pole dock. Helping hands quickly and efficiently unloaded the Beaver, and we reloaded it with the gear to be flown back to Watson Lake.

I heard the sound of perking coffee as I walked into the cook tent. No cook as such was here, but the store-bought cookies dunked in my coffee tasted just fine. I am a Swede, raised from a child on my great-grandmother's coffee bread and coffee; I became a dunker for life.

After a quick five minutes of dunking, two men and I climbed into the Beaver. The men were feeling bushed after a season away from civilization and were delighted to get out of camp. Tonight a real shower, restaurant food and clean sheets were in order. We made a downwind takeoff and had a pleasant flight back to Watson Lake.

On August 11, 12 and 13 I made several trips from Cantung into Howard's Pass, flying fuel for the helicopters and assorted camping gear into that miserable Howard's Pass strip. After collecting some more grey hairs, it was nice to prepare the Beaver FLN for a flight into Scatter River airstrip for Dempsey Collison, who had a guiding territory there. In the winter Dempsey, a handsome single young man, went south and evidently met a lot of good-looking young women. When I flew a hunting party in to his camp, usually a young lady went along as a cook or camp helper with each change of hunters. After unloading horse feed, Dempsey and I flew to Fort Nelson and back to Scatter River strip with some more supplies, after which I returned to Watson Lake.

The Snow Birds, the Canadian acrobatic jet team, flew into Watson Lake one day to put on a show. It was a nice day, and one of the pilots from the other company that flew out of Watson Lake put on a little air show of his own in a Stearman Bi-wing plane.

Down the runway and into the air went this trusty, open-cockpit antique airplane, putting on quite a show. A few seconds after touchdown, and in front of a watching crowd, the Stearman suddenly flipped over on its back. The crowd was silent, not knowing what to expect. A figure wriggled down to the ground from the upside-down position and silently walked away, never lifting his eyes from the ground.

The Stearman was nose-heavy. After the acrobatic performance, the pilot probably had his feet on the top of the rudder pedals, which were the brakes on the ground, and that would cause the ship to flip over quite suddenly. The Snow Birds put on a marvelous show of breathtaking precision acrobatics as they swooped and climbed in formation!

On August 18 Scott was with me in IBP as several mining people were on their way to Smithers, B.C. It was a beautiful flight. We stopped at Provinger Lake, Germanson Landing, Delcluz Lake and then Smithers. We landed at McClure Lake, where my flying career had begun. I had forgotten how beautiful the country was in the Bulkley Valley. The valley was a rich, deep green, and the day was warm. I felt the same peaceful feeling this place first gave me when we arrived in 1964.

We caught a cab to town, and then another cab drove us to our former log home in Driftwood Valley. The log cabin was as I remembered it – no noticeable changes except for a large window and a fence – a quiet, beautiful, peaceful setting among the pine and spruce trees. This was my first trip back in a couple years since our log home was sold.

Scott worked Sunday through Friday, six days a week, from 1:00 p.m. to 10:00 p.m. He was well liked and did an excellent job. Grant Taylor, the owner and his boss, said he was the best help they had ever hired.

Scott repaired 200-pound truck tires, serviced trucks and cars and cashed out at night. I disliked the stubborn diesel smell that clung to his clothes when he got home. We often went to the Watson Lake Hotel and used their shower.

I flew into Telegraph Creek in our Aztec CF-HIA on August 29. The mighty Stikine River flows just below the town of Telegraph Creek, B.C. The town was named by the Collins Overland Telegraph Company. Their line to Asia was to cross the Stikine River at this location. The Tahltan Indians had a village near the town site. About four miles east the Stikine River flows for 60 miles through the Grand Canyon of the Stikine, a truly remarkable and awesome area to fly through.

The Aztec HIA was back from a repair shop in Calgary, repaired to the tune of about $30,000. One of the pilots had evidently retracted the wheels before the Aztec was airborne. He nicked a prop. Instead of going around and landing, not knowing if the props and engine were badly damaged, he bellied it in, which was the wisest thing to do.

After a nice flight to Cassiar and Telegraph Creek with Scott and school officials, Scott and I sat down for breakfast at a café in Telegraph Creek. We talked about many things – the history of the town, our feelings. We then walked through the Indian graveyard and saw some Indian bones lying in the open. There were small spirit houses over most of the graves. We left, wondering deeply about who those people were and what their life had been like.

On our trip back toward Eddontenajon, the door in the Aztec HIA flew open, and it felt as though the plane would shake itself apart and fall from the sky. The passengers held on as tightly as possible to the door but were not able to close it. We landed safely in the Indian village of Iskut and shut the door. However, the day was hot. The cranky fuel-injected 290-horsepower Lycoming engines acted up when they were hot, and it was one hour before I could start them. We returned to Cassiar with the school officials and then flew to Watson Lake. Gordon Scott, our apprentice engineer, worked on the faulty door lock and told me it was okay, or so it seemed at the time.

My journal entry for August 30 reads, "Almost wrecked the Aztec. Today was another grey hair day, one of my most nerve-racking. I flew to Macmillan Pass with my son Scott to pick up a load of mining gear. The strip was 1500 to 2000 feet long and 4500 feet above sea level. Fortunately, after putting in a heavy payload, I had the sense to unload a few heavy items. This was after warming up, taxiing for takeoff and then deciding not to take an unnecessary risk. Good thinking for me this day! It no doubt saved a wrecked airplane and possibly our lives! After unloading the heavy items that were on top, I taxied to the far end of the north end of the gravel strip I applied full power, released the brakes and picked up speed rapidly as the two powerful engines propelled me toward the end of the strip. Just as I began to rotate past the point of no return, the door popped open. Not having room to stop, and knowing I would go off the end of the strip if we didn't become airborne, I somehow managed to lift the plane into the air. The flight manual says if the door comes open in a situation like this, the outcome is "doubtful" or words to that effect. We staggered into the air and down the valley. Bringing up the landing gear helped somewhat, but we struggled down the valley for many miles until I got some altitude and could breathe regularly. Scott was holding onto the door for dear life, pulling it as far shut as he could, but the air pressure kept it from closing completely. The airplane continued to buck and complain all the way home. I was angry because I was told the door had been fixed earlier. Having been very close to death, I vented my anger when we returned. A bolt-type sliding lock similar to an outhouse lock was installed, and it solved the problem."

Fall came quickly and early to Watson Lake. The trees and meadows were suddenly splashed with golds and red overnight; the season was rapidly drawing to a close. Winter would soon come…in fact, much sooner than we expected.

September 7, 9 and 10 I made fuel hauls into Howard's Pass in the Aztec HIA without too much difficulty. The strip was dry by then. Because of altitude and the heavy loads I was carrying, I noticed 85 mph was as slow as I could approach on final. Approaching slower than that resulted in buffeting, a warning that the airplane was approaching a stall.

September 10 I flew IBP into Rex Logan's hunting camp on the Keel River. Rex was a well-known and respected old-timer and one of the best big game outfitters and wranglers in this country. I flew new hunters and groceries in and other hunters out. The trip in was about 240 miles one way, a good moneymaker. But it was over the rugged Mackenzie Mountains, and it was worth every penny I made. The river landing was a bit tricky, and a mishap could occur easily on this stretch of the river. When you are a long way from civilization, special care is a must.

September 18 I made another trip to Rex Logan's camp. The season was about over, as winter could come any time, and the freeze up was drawing close. I flew several hunters out. Rex and his guides trailed the horses out to a road – about a two-week trip.

I wrote in my journal on October 5 that the weather the past ten days had turned to snow and cold in the higher elevations. I tried unsuccessfully to get into Plateau Lake, and those hunters were picked up later by a helicopter! This lake was thinly frozen, so I was unable to land there. I flew skis into the Scatter River airstrip 20 miles distant. I was also able to fly into a small lake on floats in IBP to pick up some German hunters. A small bay was unfrozen. I told them to leave all their belongings including toothbrushes. My red Beaver IBP performed superbly, and we were off the water and into the air before we hit the ice. One of the Germans who was a pilot pounded my back and said, "Good, good!" It had been four months exactly since I had made the last trip on skis – a short summer.

There were constant reminders that we really were "braving the untamed wilderness." This fall a hunter I flew in earlier to a hunting camp got lost and was never found. He went ahead of the guide on the trail and said he could find his own way back. Another man, a prospector, was also lost and never found. A pilot dropped him off at Divide Lake, and two months later I flew in the Royal Canadian Mounted Police in the Beaver on floats. We flew low, but no trace was found, and fresh snow and ice on the lake prevented our landing. We found his neatly set up camp, but no prospector. The scene was stark and etched deeply in my mind. We recognized the tragic end to this man's dream. In 1983 his thick glasses, some tattered clothing and wristwatch were found near Divide Lake. Darrell Nelson, who outfitted in that area, said the watch began ticking. He thought that a grizzly bear might have killed the prospector, but no one will ever know for sure. A guide and a camp helper from two separate camps lost their lives that fall in accidents, as well.

This was a season of tough flying for me. I felt very fortunate and lucky that I experienced no accidents and still had my hide.

On a typical trip into the "white knuckle strip: at Howard's Pass, I was carrying explosives on the Beaver. As usual, a crosswind was coming down the mountain, tending to push me off the strip into a draw. As I bounced around the curve, the wind and centrifugal force and the sloping strip pushed me toward the draw. I bounced to the very edge and rode the ridge along the drop-off! Full left aileron, left rudder, and we somehow stayed on the edge until the plane slowed. At that time I got it back on the main strip, but I mentally expected a wreck at any moment. I once made four passes at that strip before landing.

Flying late in the fall when it was snowing made navigation very difficult. In a snowstorm, if you followed a river that was open, you had a dark object to fly over and to help keep your horizon in perspective. If the river was frozen and everything was white, it got very hazardous. Then you were at risk of a whiteout condition when you lose all visual contact. We flew VFR (visual flight rules) in our operations. The airplanes were not equipped for instrument flight. Jim Thibaudeau and I had instrument ratings, but without navigation equipment in the airplanes we were unable to make instrument approaches. He and I often talked about getting out of flying; we felt we were close to being burned out and were pushing our luck. The season of long hours without days off and the many close calls we had in this type of flying caused us to think about another kind of work before long. Jim had opened a sporting goods store and was also going to work with Ron Holly, putting water and sewer lines into new homes.

As the season drew to an end after many flights into Howard's Pass and some other rather hazardous trips, I felt ready to give it up, at least part of the time. However, I still had a love for flying, so there was a conflict. Of course, after a long and busy season with your last few trips in winter-like snow conditions, you get superstitious and hope your luck and good fortune holds until the last trip is completed.

Jim Close signed my logbook October 2, 1974: "Time logged to date certified," and he put the Watson Lake Flying Service stamp above his signature. I left Watson Lake and began the long drive down the Alaska Highway. It was a demanding season, and I felt as though this might be my last season of flying the bush. I was drained and looking forward to a long rest, away from flying.

Our Piper Aztec HIA that I flew often. I made most of the chartered flights
booked for this plane. I was the only one in the company that had flown
an Aztec as I took my training for the Airlines Transport Pilot license in
it. It had a 290 HP instead of the normal 250 HP fuel injected engine and
cruised about 200 knots. Scott went with me on the second trip and got the
chance to fly it. It was a nice airplane to fly with lots of power and a good
payload. But Scott and I had a close call when the door popped open more
than once until it was fixed.

Chapter 9

LAST SEASON IN THE YUKON

On December 20, 1974, Scott and I drove to Seattle. Scott began gliding lessons near Issaquah on a grass strip and soloed on the third day of flying lessons. The instructor and I watched Scott make his solo approach to the small grass strip to land but, because of other traffic in the pattern, he had to circle first. Because there was no engine, we were concerned that he might not have enough altitude left to make the field, and we both tried to put on a good face as though there was no problem.

Scott handled the situation like a pro. He made an extra circle but stayed close enough to the field to make the landing without a problem. He made a good landing, but because one wing was a bit low on landing, the instructor said, "Scott, you're part Chinese – One Wing Lo." Scott was all smiles, and I was one proud father. Scott was 14 years old, which was the minimum age to solo in a glider. Minimum to solo in a power plane was 16. He made 21 flights in all and paid for them with the money he made working for Grant Taylor's truck stop and service station in Watson Lake. One day while I was waiting for Scott to finish his flight lesson I watched a man in a parachute land on the grass runway. His parachute came down on the engine and propeller of a Cessna 150 tow plane that was ready to take off with engines running. The pilot was looking back at the glider. The propeller was pulling the man in the parachute to the plane. Just then the pilot turned around and saw what was happening with a look of horror on his face. The parachute wrapped tightly around the prop causing the engine to quit, just a few feet before the man would have been hit by the prop. I can still see that close call in my mind's eye.

After Scott finished his glider flying, we headed for Spokane to spend the holidays with relatives. Scott had to return to Prince George in early January for school, but I had a trip planned to visit him in mid-February.

I had a nice visit with Scott in February. We spent the afternoon at Prince George Airport and looked at a sharp DC-3 used by Northern Thunderbird for hauling passengers to Penticton. We also watched some cross-country skiers and discussed world problems but reached no real solutions. Scott had a mature insight into life and raised some interesting thoughts. Over breakfast the next day we discussed Luscomb Silvars and the possibility of purchasing one and installing a 150-horsepower Lycoming engine, flaps and floats. I so enjoyed making plans with him.

I made a trip south to spend a week in the Arizona sun. After visiting Yuma, Tucson and Phoenix, I went to Las Vegas where I lost $30. Good thing I had only a little money on me. I bought a leather flight jacket, pilot's logbook, maps and other items for my position as a pilot in Sitka, Alaska where I had been offered a position. March 9 I caught an Alaska Airlines flight for Sitka. I spent a nice day but somehow didn't feel comfortable about the job, and I decided to return to Seattle. The flying in the area was usually marginal at best, due to bad weather along the coast, and it just didn't feel right. Turning it down was the right decision. I spent my 37th birthday in Spokane, Washington on April 2, 1975.

Near the end of April I began packing personal belongings and, of course, my blue down-filled sleeping bag that I had bought many years ago from Tommy Walker, which was always part of my survival gear in the red Beaver, and left for Watson Lake. After three long days and nights driving and sleeping along the Alaska Highway, I arrived safely at Watson Lake for another season of flying for Watson Lake Flying Service.

On May 20, 1975, the Mercedes-Benz people arrived. The owner of the Mercedes Corporation would arrive later for a hunt into Frank Cooke's area. These people were going to be making several flights into the camp to make sure it was set up the way their boss wanted it. They chartered the Aztec CF-HIA to fly into Frank Cooke's main camp on Scoop Lake.

The trip to Scoop Lake took 40 minutes one way. I did almost all of the flying in the Aztec HIA, which I really enjoyed. Leaving the Beaver and climbing into the Aztec was like getting out of a truck and into a Cadillac with cushy seats and almost 200 mph cruise. It was interesting to have two engines to play with instead of one. The flight back to Watson Lake was pleasant; the days were getting long, and the weather was sunny and mild.

I flew them back into Scoop Lake again on May 22 and 23 with the Aztec before they were satisfied all was okay. Later on, the son of the family that owned Mercedes-Benz arrived in Scoop Lake. He told Frank he wanted a certain tame goose Frank had for dinner. Frank replied, "It's not for sale."

"I'll give you $500 for that goose."

"It's still not for sale!" The goose went on to live its pampered lifestyle.

"White Knuckle Strip," Howard's Pass, came back into my life on May 25 and again on May 27. I safely flew the red Beaver on wheels into the pass with a load of groceries, camp supplies and mail.

Gary Moore, the new owner of Skook's ranch and hunting area, chartered me to fly into the ranch at Terminus Mountain. It was not a great strip, but the Aztec got in and out without any problem. Gary was an interesting man. He had done well for himself in the lumbering business. At this time he was in his 30s and really enjoyed the guiding business. He had a Cessna 185 on floats that he flew into some of the lakes in his guiding area.

Mitchell B-25s in Watson Lake? Yes, indeed! Two flew into the airport to be on call for the Forest Service in the event of forest fires. They had been converted to water bombers. Since they were a co-pilot short, they offered me the position. They assured me it would be only while they were in the area, and it should not interfere with my charter flying. They would check me out give me an endorsement on my license, and provide free meals if I acted as co-pilot on a B-25 with a shark's grin painted on the nose. This B-25, CF-MWC, which I flew, reminded me of Chinault's Flying Tigers.

Of course, I agreed and started logging time on this type of airplane. The B-25 was the first plane to bomb Tokyo. This mission was handled off a carrier under the leadership of Jimmy Doolittle.

I logged 2.2 hours on the B-25 June 9, 2.3 hours in two separate flights June 11, and 2 hours on June 15. My log book entry for June 15, 1975 read, "Time for North American B-25: Certified Correct. L. Harrold, North Western Air Lease Ltd. (Chief Pilot)." The Department of Transportation put an endorsement on my commercial license for the B-25.

The engines were rated at 1800 horsepower each, and when they idled they gave you a good shaking. It was a beautiful airplane to fly, honest and forgiving. The B-25 pilots from back East, what I called the flat lands, were not used to flying in the mountains and did not know this area. We were notified by the Department of Transportation that a large helicopter was lost. They asked if we would help in the search and agreed to furnish free gas if we would.

Because I knew the country and was used to flying in the mountains, the captain in my B-25 let me do the flying. I flew as I always did in the mountains. I tucked one wing up close to the mountain, where there was some lift on one side of the valley so if I needed to I could make a 180-degree turn safely. The captain eyed the side of the mountain and me with a quizzical look but said nothing. We logged many hours but were unable to find the helicopter. As far as I know, it was never located.

Because the pilot and co-pilot of the B-25s didn't have float endorsements, we let them fly our Super Cub. I gave them several hours of dual instructions and endorsed their logbooks for float flying when I thought they could handle the seaplane safely.

In Canada, any commercial pilot with a float endorsement can give a float endorsement to another pilot. I had an instructor rating but didn't really need it to legally give them their float ratings. They enjoyed the float flying, and I was thrilled to get a free endorsement and several hours in a B-25. When I was flying the B-25 through the mountains I went back in time and pretended I was in World War II on a bombing mission.

We practiced and demonstrated water bombing at the airport on June 20 for 30 minutes. It was exciting to drop on a target and pull up and away, light now that the hold was empty. It must have been impressive from the ground because of the size and noise of these wonderful birds from another age.

One day they were called to another location, and that was the last I saw of the planes or pilots. The memories are still vivid, climbing up into the belly of the B-25 in a chin up configuration, cranking up the engines and roaring off into the wild blue yonder with a tremendous noise.

I made two trips safely into Howard's Pass with the red Beaver on June 15, two trips on June 17, two trips on June 21 and one on June 23. On June 24 Scott and I prepared for a most interesting trip in the Aztec.

Some mining people wanted us to pick them up at Cantung (Tungsten) in the Northwest Territories and fly then first to Farrow and then Dawson City where we would overnight. On the following day we would fly them to another mining camp for a few hours, then drop the men off at Whitehorse before returning to Watson Lake. It was a nice trip, a good moneymaker, and I would be able to take my son along.

The flight to Cantung was 130 air miles. We picked up the Hyland River near Stewart Lake and followed it most of the way. The gravel road to Cantung intercepted the Hyland River about 22 miles north of Stewart Lake, and we followed it into Cantung. Besides being a good landmark to follow, it could be used as an emergency airstrip if we developed engine trouble or had weather problems.

Flying in this country without floats made me feel somewhat naked. There were so few places to land a wheel plane. With floats there are countless lakes or rivers; even a meadow is okay and can be used without much of a problem on floats, because you have a large surface with the float bottoms and are not as likely to flip over as you would with a wheel plane.

Thinking of Dawson City, I went back to my childhood days when I read Jack London's *The Call of the Wild*, listened on the radio to "Sergeant Preston of the Northwest Mounted Police" and his wonder dog King and stories of my grandfather's uncle who left his store and headed for the gold fields in the last century.

Dawson City sits at the junction of the Klondike and Yukon Rivers. In 1975 it was a town of about 800 people, but it had once numbered over 25,000 when the Klondikers came between 1896 and 1899. Silent buildings remain of a once lively, rip-roaring town, where saloons and gambling casinos kept busy and where the motto was "Never refuse a man a drink or kick a dog." A few buildings were still in use, and some had been renovated. The original post office was still in use, as was Diamond Tooth Gertie's, a gambling hall that offered roulette, black jack, can-can girls and bingo. As far as I knew, it was the only place in Canada that allowed legalized gambling.

Gold was discovered ten miles southeast of here on Bonanza Creek, a tributary of the Klondike River, in 1896 by George Camack, Skookum Jim and Tagish Charlie. Word of the gold reached the outside in 1897, and the Klondike Stampede began.

We approached the town of Cantung from the south. The gravel airstrip just south of town was clearly visible as I came through the pass following the road. Rounding out near the end of the strip we were soon down and taxiing to the pickup truck that waited for us with the mining officials who would be our companions for the next couple of days.

The two gentlemen climbed aboard. We taxied to the north end of the strip and accelerated down the runway. Because of a good payload and a little higher altitude, it took longer to get airborne, and we used about 1500 feet of the strip before we were airborne.

Our first destination was Faro, 170 miles due west. Soon Pelly Lakes in the Yukon Territory slipped under our wings, and then we crossed the old Canal Road and picked up the Campbell Highway west of there and followed it into Faro, where we landed on a good gravel strip near town.

After fueling and waiting a few hours for our clients to take care of their business there, we were once again airborne, our destination Dawson City. This was Scott's first trip to Dawson, and he was excited. I once flew the Beaver on floats there, landing on the mighty Yukon River.

We followed the Pelly River on a northwest course, cross-country flying over this wilderness. North of Pelly Crossing we picked up the gravel Klondike Highway and had a road under us to Dawson City. Flying over Dawson City, we circled the gravel strip and soon were on final, landing into the wind from the southwest. We touched down on a fairly soft surface, a good ending for this day's flying.

After tying down HIA we managed to catch a ride to town, where we had a room booked in the motel. But guess what – somehow they had us booked for the next day, and they had no available rooms. It was at the peak of the tourist season, and we couldn't seem to find a room anywhere. Someone suggested Black Mike's place, an old, tall, skinny two-story gold rush original from the 1800s era. It was out of town and a good mile's walk.

The building looked like something from another time zone, but we were glad to get a room. They even had inside plumbing down the hall. We had a large room for the four of us, with three beds. Scott and I agreed to share the double bed.

It was light outside all night, and we didn't feel like going to bed yet, so we walked back to town. We walked to Robert Service's log cabin, the old hospital and saw many of the original buildings.

Scott and I went to the Gaslight Follies Theater, which had been restored to its original condition. We watched a play about the Klondike days. Because we were in Dawson City and the buildings were the genuine originals, we were able to feel that special time of long ago. The acting was superb, and the audience was soon into the play. Laughter seemed to shake the building, bringing life from that era into the theater. Romance, life and death were acted out in a light comedy of the far North.

Scott decided to go back to the hotel at around midnight, but the rest of us wanted to visit the downtown area that was lively with tourists and the local people who lived there. We returned to the Black Mike Hotel at about three in the morning, only to face yet another unexpected setback. Scott had locked the door, and he had the only key. We banged on the door to try to arouse him from a deep sleep, but finally gave up. One of the men climbed into the bathtub to try to get some sleep, and the other stretched out on the floor. I told them that someday we'd recall this event and laugh about it, but of course we were dead tired and didn't see any humor in it just yet.

Finally I decided to go outside and see if I could get up to the outside window and maybe wake Scott. I found a ladder and was able to get to the window, which was close to the bed that Scott was sleeping in. Scott broke an eardrum in a swimming accident and didn't hear well in one ear, and of course he was sleeping on his good ear. I banged on the window for a while, and Scott finally woke up and let us in. It was about 4:00 a.m. by now, and we got about three hours of sleep before getting up, eating breakfast and departing for the mining town of Clinton Creek about 45 miles northwest. There we spent a few hours and had a good meal before departing for Whitehorse.

Flying on a southeast heading we picked up the Klondike Highway at Minto and followed it, flying over Yukon Crossing, Carmacks – passing just west of Lake Labarge where the cremation of Sam McGee took place, the event immortalized in one of Robert Service's poems – and on into the Whitehorse airport.

After unloading their gear, we hopped in, and I cranked up both engines and taxied out near the end of the runway to do my preflight takeoff checklist. I got clearance from the tower to take off. We accelerated rapidly, because we were lightly loaded, and soared into the clear Yukon sky. Shortly after takeoff, the door popped open, since the sliding bolt lock wasn't completely closed, and the regular handle door lock never did work properly. I quickly opened a vent to equalize the pressure, and we were able to lock it. The flight back was pleasant, and the weather was sunny and warm, so we relaxed, cherishing this adventure that we shared. I let Scott take control on the co-pilot's side, and he flew part of the way home with a smile on his face.

On July 1 I flew the Beaver FLN to Little Dal Lake, then to the Nahanni River for Darrell Nelson's South Nahanni Outfitters.

It was July 12, and I was waiting at the float base office for the weather to improve. A system of bad weather had us grounded here at the lake, but it was moving north and had improved a bit. I had a trip booked into Macmillan Pass with the Beaver to fly some camp supplies in for a mining camp. Sometimes waiting for the weather to clear was one of the hardest things for me. The trips continued to pile up, and the pressures built as the various camps needed food and supplies. The camps did not always understand why we couldn't fly in when the weather at their locations was good.

Some of the camps were 100 to 300 miles away, and the weather between us was often unflyable. We did our best, however, to keep the supplies and people moving into the various camps as close to the scheduled flights as possible. It was not a lot of fun to sit at some isolated place and wait out the weather. It was much better to wait at the base and go another day.

By late afternoon the worst of the storm seemed to have passed through, and I decided to head north to see if I could get to Macmillan Pass. I followed the Frances River north, flying close to the Campbell Highway until I reached the west side of Frances Lake and then headed on a northeast course cross country in a fairly direct line to the Canal Road and Macmillan Pass.

On wheels instead of floats, I felt naked. The many lakes and swamps made a good emergency landing easy with floats, but with wheels the prospects were poor for a safe landing in most areas along this route.

Visibility was okay, although the ceiling was still low. I could see the Canal Road ahead and was soon flying parallel to it, following it to the airstrip. I relaxed somewhat, as I had a road that could be used as an emergency strip if I had to set it down.

Up ahead and under my port wing the strip at Macmillan Pass came into view, running north and south. The wind was from the south, so my downwind leg was parallel to the strip in a northerly heading, and final was into the wind on the south runway.

I quickly unloaded the Beaver, as I wanted to get back before the weather deteriorated again. It was about 150 miles home to Watson Lake, and the weather looked black and threatening to the south and was beginning to lower again. Flying over Frances Lake 70 miles from home, the clouds and the ground met a few miles south of the lake over the Frances River. Having no other choice, I made a steep turn and did a quick 180. The weather behind me where I had been minutes before formed a solid barrier to the ground, and I had to fly over the east arm of the lake.

I was restricted to a small area, and all I could do was circle and circle. My situation was becoming critical. The gas gauges all showed empty, the needles bouncing off the E mark on the three belly tanks, and the darkness descended to envelop my small craft. I prepared to crash. There was a couple who lived in a cabin below, and I planned to set down in the trees or water, thinking they would help me get out of the plane if I was injured.

Circling up the side of one mountain on the east side of the lake, I was hoping to get a better view of the mountains to the west where I could find a hole and land on the road beyond. My airspeed dropped to a dangerously low 45 miles per hour, but I happened to glance down before a stall occurred and quickly lowered the nose to resume the 70 miles per hour slow flight speed that I was flying with partial flaps. In bad weather, slowing down and using flaps gives you more time and also enables you to turn in a smaller radius if the situation requires.

To the west I could see a little light above the mountain ridge where there was a saddle. Skimming over the treetops I was able to get through and slip down the other side of the mountain, fly over the west arm of the lake and to the road beyond. A straight stretch of road appeared, and I flew parallel to it as I descended, giving it a close look. The road ran north-south just west of the lake. I was flying south, to the right side of the road, intending to land in a northerly direction. Slowing down, I started lowering the flaps and began a 180-degree steep, descending turn to the left, approaching the landing site with full flaps and an airspeed of about 60 miles per hour. Complete concentration was necessary, as this was probably the only chance I would get. It was a moonless night, the gauges showed empty, and the road was extremely narrow. Touchdown was smooth, and the Beaver rolled to a stop up a small incline. Had we been off the center slightly or touched the brakes, the Beaver probably would have been wrecked, as the road bank was steep and there was a good drop-off to the bottom.

The airplane was safe, and I was alive. The relief was overwhelming, and I didn't care whether I ever flew another plane. Using the landing light, I taxied north on the road for about two miles until I found a place wide enough to park the Beaver off the road for the night. I stretched out my sleeping bag behind the pilot's seat and soon fell into an exhausted and very much appreciated sleep.

Jim Thibaudeau was close to my location here on this road. He was down on Frances Lake in the Beech 18 flying freight into Lori Bliss's area in the Northwest Territories but had been holding for the weather. I knew Jim would have gas, so I walked down to the lake at the end of a dirt road. Jim and the other people there were surprised to see me. We loaded up a 45-gallon drum on a pickup. After I had breakfast with some people from Watson Lake who were camping here, I left with Jim and one other man who guided for Lori Bliss at about 9:00 a.m.

After I fueled up the Beaver, Jim walked in one direction and the guide walked in the other direction to stop any traffic while I took off in the red Beaver. I warmed up the Beaver, went through my checklist and then applied full power. IBP, being light, lifted quickly off the narrow dirt road, and I headed south to Watson Lake, about 100 miles away. The weather was good, and the bosses, curious as to why I was a day late, were glad to know I was okay. Add another to the list of close calls that almost ended my flying career.

The very next day I had a trip to Howard's Pass. Two days later on July 15 I made my last wheel flight in the red Beaver to Howard's Pass and returned to Watson Lake safely. On July 19 I began flying this Beaver on floats, as we took the wheels off due to the demand for another floatplane. The hunting season was approaching, and the hunters would soon be arriving and would have to be flown on floats to the various lakes in B.C., the Yukon and Northwest Territories.

Over the next few days I flew into Burnt Rose Lake, Mayfield Lake and Wolverine Lake, and made a trip in the Aztec to move a camp from the Liard airstrip. I flew through a flock of small birds upon landing, but no damage to the plane was done. I made several more trips in HIA to Howard's Pass and several in the red Beaver to places like Summit Lake and Terminus Mountain on the Ketchika River, Misty Lake and Sandpile Lake. A long day for Frank Cooke, mostly with the red Beaver to Scoop and Denetiah Lakes, finished out the month of July, logging 8.5 hours in the red Beaver.

In August I flew into Tobally, Misty, Tom, Hyland, Provinger, Sandpile, Deadwood, Stone Axe, Ervin, Flat, Mink, Junion, Daughny, Muncho, Brown, Mayfield, Tootsi, Meeting, Plateau, Crooked, Colt, Scoop, Island, Forsburg, Moodie and Boulder lakes. As usual, there were trips to Howard's Pass, Terminus Mountain and other airstrip camps and small towns. September followed much the same routine.

The next couple of days I flew into Plateau, Sandpile, Dease and Glacier lakes. From the 6th through the 21st I flew the red Beaver, mostly for outfitters as the hunting season was drawing to a close, into dozens of lakes: Junkers, Netson, Mink, Goodwin, Swan, Ice, McCaully, Daughney, Marker, Provinger, Ogden, Scoop, Colt, Sandpile, Misty, Brown, Whitefish, Pike, Meeting and more.

On September 22 I flew the Aztec to Stewart, B.C. located at the head of the Portland Canal 300 miles southeast of Watson Lake, only a few minutes' flying time north of Alice Arm, B.C., the destination of my first commercial trip with a paying passenger in 1967 when I started flying for Omineca Air Services nine years ago.

Glaciers tower over Stewart, and it was quite a drop as I flew direct and came over the mountains. Then the town appeared far below, only a short distance west of Stevens Lake, where I once flew out the world record grizzly bear in Omineca Air Service's Cessna 185, CF-OXE. Rex Handcock shot that bear with a bow and arrow in 1978 at the headwater of the Kispiox River, which was the river we lived on when we first moved to Canada. Memories flooded back: that seemed like a long time ago, a distant life, and it seemed so strange the way that time and events had flown.

On September 25 I flew the Aztec to Frank Cooke's Scoop Lake airstrip and on to Terminus Mountain airstrip at Skook's old ranch and returned to Watson Lake, logging in 1.5 hours. Another trip of 1.7 hours the same day became the last flight logged in my favorite airplane of all time, that beautiful *"Red Beaver"!*

On the 26th I flew again into Frank Cooke's camp at Scoop Lake in the Aztec, and later in the day flew the same airplane to the Titina airstrip.

My last day of flying for Watson Lake Flying Service was September 27, 1975 flying the Aztec HIA to the Titina airstrip, logging 1.2 hours. On these last trips of the season I became superstitious. It was this time of year when the weather got bad. Snowstorms and icing conditions prevailed and made for hazardous flying. I was tired after a busy flying season and was flying on the edge of my seat, hoping for a safe landing.

Goodbyes were said. I told the pilots I flew with and my employers that this was my final season; I was planning to get into another line of work and felt it was time to make a change. I felt exhausted after the close calls flying into Howard's Pass and Macmillan Pass this past summer and was looking forward to going south and beginning a new career.

After packing my 1972 blue Volvo, I left Watson Lake on the journey south and new adventures. I felt fortunate and relieved to have the flying season safely behind me.

The trip down the Alaska Highway was wet and the road muddy, due to heavy fall rains. The Yukon slipped away, and a new season in my life began.

A few weeks after I left the Yukon I received a call from an employee at Watson Lake Flying Service who said, "Jim Thibaudeau and two hunters he was flying in the Beech 18 were killed." Jim left Rose Lake in northern British Columbia with the hunters and encountered severe icy conditions. Jim landed on Solitaire Lake about 40 miles south of Watson Lake to wait out the bad weather. After taking off from

Solitaire Lake Jim again encountered severe icy conditions and crashed, killing him and the two hunters.

Jim was a good family man and left a beautiful young wife and two small children. I was told that over his grave is a Beech 18 propeller. I flew with Jim for about seven years, both at B.C. Yukon Air Service and Watson Lake Flying Service. He was a very good bush pilot, friendly, kind and well respected.

In July 1993 while making a video of the north, I watched the red Beaver land and take off of Watson Lake with some hunters. As I watched it disappear, I said "so long, my friend," and had a feeling that this would be the last time I saw the red Beaver. A few years later I received a call from Watson Lake Flying Service saying that the red Beaver crashed. A pilot they hired from England was hauling some hunters' gear in northern British Columbia and crashed in bad weather on the side of a mountain and was killed. A helicopter pilot out of Dease Lake B.C. called me and said he flew the red Beaver's engine out.

The years I spent flying my favorite float plane of all time, the red Beaver CF IBP with my son Scott as co-pilot in the Yukon has given me a treasure of memories of a special time when we were young.

Scott's first solo flight in a glider near Issaquah, Washington at age 14. December 1974.

Scott getting ready for another flight in the glider.

Scott's solo flight at the age of 14 in this glider near Issaquah, Washington in December 1974.

Scott and Larry on the right with some Canadian Government Park officials by the Red Beaver along the South Nahanni River, Northwest Territories. The park officials were mapping out the future Nahanni National Park which it later became. It is 2-1/2 times larger than Yellowstone Park. We are about 1/2 mile from Virginia Falls, twice as high as Niagara Falls.

The Old Hudson Bay trading post at Telegraph Creek, B.C. that Larry used to fly into in the 1970's. He also flew into Ft. Babine, B.C. with the mail and it also had a Hudson Bay Trading Post that traded with the Indians in the '60s and '70s.

Diamond Tooth Gertie's Gambling Hall from the Klondike Gold Rush period, Dawson City, Yukon. Scott and Larry visited the establishment and also watched a play about that time period of 1897-1899, at the Dawson City Gaslight Follies in 1975.

A man with a strong Scottish accent was quoting some of Robert Services poems by heart! Service was the great poet of the Klondike Gold Rush and this was his cabin. Jack London's cabin is about 100 feet east of here. Jack London wrote The Call of the Wild.

Scott and Larry watched a play at the Dawson City Gaslight Follies in 1975!

Chapter 10

AFTER OUR YUKON FLYING ADVENTURES

Scott soloed in a Piper J-3 Cub on his 16th birthday at Henley Aerodrome in Athol, Idaho, and I watched this flight with other family members. It was exciting to watch my son have the freedom to fly alone in the sky, and it was a smooth flight.

Kathy and Scott moved from Prince George, B.C. to Bellevue, Washington. Scott went to Lake Sammamish High School where he played football, wrestled and threw the discus and holds the high school record in that event.

After graduating from high school, Scott moved to Spokane and lived with me. After my last flying season in the Yukon, I returned to my hometown of Spokane and for the next 18 years was in the real estate business.

Scott and I continued to fly together. We rented a Cessna 185 on floats and flew off the Spokane River beside Felts Field and in a Cessna 172 off Felts Field. One of my favorite places to fly the floatplane was the beautiful retirement home of my sister Nancy and her husband, Doug Furlott, beside the Pend Oreille River, a few miles north of Newport, Washington. One day I flew their oldest son, Jon, to Upper Priest Lake. Their other son, Andy, and his wife, Nikki, have two sons, Connor and Lyam, and Nancy and Doug are happy grandparents. Nancy has always been a special part of my life, and we are close. She is a wonderful sister, and our parents, Jeanne and Velmur Whitesitt, gave us a loving home to grow up in. Our kind easy going brother, Bob Whitesitt, passed away on June 2, 2008. He was honorably discharged from the U.S. Navy Reserve.

Scott began building houses in the Spokane area, and we bought a new house together in Greenacres, Washington, which was in a nice country area.

Scott decided he wanted to become an architect and went to Washington State University where he graduated with a degree in architecture in 1986. While attending WSU Scott spent the summers of 1981 and 1982 as a builder. In 1981 he built a triplex for the schoolteachers at the Indian village at Angoon, Alaska and a gymnasium at the school on Admiralty Island. He hired four Indians to help him construct the building.

One day while fishing for halibut in the ocean he heard shotgun shots. Later he found out fishermen killed the large halibuts, some weighing several hundred pounds, because they would thrash around on the deck and cause a lot of damage. Scott went deer hunting with an Indian from the village. Scott was going to start a campfire, and the Indian said, "Let me show you an old Indian trick for starting a fire with one match. He poured gas on the wood and started the fire with one match!

In the summer of 1982 Scott and a few other carpenters finished the construction of a Forest Service bunkhouse on Chicagof Island, Alaska. He said there were a large number of grizzly bears, and they would follow the men, beside the trail on the way to work. Scott carried a .44 magnum but never had to use it. The bears were just curious. Scott said the men would watch the bears at a dump. There was a logging camp on the island and they had a helicopter.

He took flying lessons while attending WSU and made some solo cross-country flights. Shortly after graduation, Scott married his beautiful wife Stacy on January 18, 1987!

Scott designed and built a unique two-story country home along Rathdrum Creek 1-1/2 miles north of Rathdrum, Idaho, where they still live. Kathy lives on Lower Twin Lakes, about four miles from Scott's home, where she retired.

In 2005 Scott designed the Pasco Sherman Indian School and dormitory at the St. Mary Mission near Omak, Washington for the Colville Federated Tribe.

One of his projects was designing the new YMCA/YWCA building in Spokane. It was the first time they were in the same building. Scott and a partner designed the Aqua Center at Fairchild Air Force Base Survival School. He designed the Four Season Home and Garden Center at McCord Air Force Base. When my book *Higher Than Eagles, Spokane's World War II Pilots* was published, I spent five days living on the base autographing books in the building he designed. Scott did a similar project at Hickam Air Force Base in Hawaii and received a National Honor Award from General Lupa in Virginia for his design.

Jim Goetz, my high school buddy and best friend, died on December 21, 2016. We fulfilled our youthful dreams when we immigrated to Canada in 1964, built our cabins in the far north and fished and hunted for food. We experienced some great adventures including a ski-plane crash on a frozen wilderness lake. Jim was a devout Christian and a pastor. Jim had MS for over 30 years and now he's pain free. I'm looking forward to a happy reunion with Jim, family, and friends in Heaven with my Lord and Saviour, Jesus! God has richly blessed my life with a wonderful family and friends. My favorite song is *Amazing Grace*! My favorite Bible verse is John 3:16. *"For God so loved the world that He gave His one and only Son, that whoever believes in Him shall not perish but have eternal life."*

Scott and Stacy have three grown children who all graduated from Lakeland High School in Rathdrum and were active in sports. They are wonderful parents and excellent role models for their children.

Daniel, the oldest, married his beautiful wife Jordan on July 23, 2016. He is thinking about building their home across the creek from his Dad and Mom's place.

Daniel at 6'5" tall was a very good athlete playing baseball and football in high school. He was offered a scholarship to play football at Whitworth University but graduated from the University of Idaho and received a scholarship from the State of Idaho to go to dental school at Creighton University in Omaha Nebraska. In April 2019 Daniel passed his board exams and is a licensed dentist. He graduated from Creighton University. It was fun watching Daniel and my two other grandchildren play sports as they were growing up. When Daniel was 4-years-old, we went fishing and he caught his first fish. While taking a photo of Daniel holding up the fish he caught, he was shaking, and I knew he was going to be a lifetime fisherman like my grandfather was who taught me how to fish. I took Daniel to a course on tying flies, and he ties his own flies and is an expert fly fisherman. He and Jordan fish together, and they each try to catch the largest fish. When Daniel was about five years old, we were hiking on the Mineral Ridge Trail above Lake Coeur d'Alene and met a couple on the trail with a grown dog and a puppy. They told Daniel he could pick up the puppy. While holding the pup Daniel looked up and said, "Grandpa, how can I get a puppy?" and I said, "We will work on it." I found a good kennel in the Spokane Valley with a litter of yellow labs. Daniel picked out a male, which we purchased. The children named him Hunter, and this kind loving dog and the children grew up together.

Kaitlyn, the second oldest child, graduated from Idaho State University in Biomedical Science and has been accepted into medical school, at the University of Utah and will begin classes on August 12, 2019. Her goal is to become a doctor. She is about 6' tall and earned a scholarship in track, pole vaulting and running at the University. She holds the record in pole-vaulting at Lakeland High School. Kaitlyn is a very good writer and has a gift for writing stories. She is a beautiful young woman with a warm, caring spirit and will make a very good doctor!

Gavin, the youngest child is 6'4". He was named the outstanding defensive lineman in the 4A league his high school was in. He was a walk on his first year of football at the University of Idaho. He was #96 on the University of Idaho Vandals football team, and he received a scholarship to play football and graduated in 2017 in economics. He is now enrolled in a Masters program in Statistics at the University. Gavin will be a teacher's assistant in 2019 which will pay for his tuition. Gavin, like his sister, is a good writer and great storyteller. When he was about 4-years-old I would take him to the Dockside Restaurant at the Coeur d'Alene Resort Hotel to eat. After dinner in the winter we would sit by the fireplace in the lobby and tell stories. At first I would tell stories about my Yukon flying and about flying the Beaver and meeting grizzly bears. But soon Gavin would tell stories about his adventure flying the Beaver float plane and his meeting with grizzly bears, and he began developing the characters in his stories. One day Gavin and I were hiking my favorite, Liberty Creek Trail by Liberty Lake where we have our huggin' trees. I noticed he was far behind, so I stopped and waited for him to catch up and see what he was doing. He was carrying a stick and said, "Oh, I shot a polar bear on the trail." My three grandchildren and I did a lot of kayaking together, sometimes fishing from the kayaks.

At age 13 Gavin told me he was interested in flying, so we drove to the Deer Park Airport for Gavin's first flying lesson in a glider. Later Gavin started to take lessons in a Cessna 172 at Felts Field. On his first lesson I sat in the back seat and Gavin in the left front pilot's seat and the instructor in the right front seat. Gavin was short then and sat on some cushions so he could see over the panel to fly. He made the takeoff and then flew the plane over his home near Rathdrum. On the flight back to Felts Field we flew over Newman Lake, and Gavin was flying relaxed like a seasoned pilot and made a good landing.

Later Gavin took flying lessons in floatplanes. His first lesson on float flying was at Hayden Lake in a Piper J-3 Cub. His instructor said Gavin was a natural pilot and said, "I have pilots with 1,000 hours come to me to learn how to fly a float plane, and Gavin does a better job. Whatever I ask him to do, he does it!"

One beautiful summer day Gavin and I each flew the Beaver floatplane N2106K off beautiful Lake Coeur d'Alene where I spent my boyhood summers fishing with my grandfather at his lake cabin. Gavin's mother, Stacy, and I sat in a middle seat as her son advanced the throttle, and we flew off the lake. Gavin made a smooth happy landing in the world's best bush pilot plane, the de Havilland Beaver float plane!

Scott soloed in this Piper J-3 Cub on his 16th birthday, January 25, 1975 at Henley Aerodrome in Athol, Idaho.

The Furlott family. From the left: Jon in back, Amy, Doug, Nancy, Andy, and his wife, Nikki. Nancy has been a wonderful sister and we are close. Doug and Nancy built their dream retirement home along the Pend Oreille River

Jon's first float plane ride. Jon Furlott and Larry Whitesitt were getting ready to fly from Sister Nancy Furlott's home on the Pend Oreille River to upper Priest Lake in this Cessna 185 float plane.

Larry's sister Nancy Furlott and her son, Andy, standing in front of the Cessna 185 Seaplane that Larry flew to their home located along the Pend Orielle River about 7 miles north of Newport, Washington in 1988.

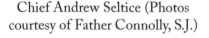

Chief Andrew Seltice (Photos courtesy of Father Connolly, S.J.)

Chief Joseph Seltice with his granddaughter, Adrianna.

Coeur d'Alene Indians

In the early 1990s, I was privileged to have a happy 43-year reunion with two lovely women who were my friends and playmates (Doty and Adrianna) when we were children in the 1940s. They lived in my grandfather's neighborhood with their grandfather, Chief Joseph Seltice, who was the last chief of the Coeur d'Alene Indians. Joseph was a kind grandfather and his grandchildren adored him.

Joseph's father, Chief Andrew Seltice, lived in the Spokane Valley in the 1850s, before the white settlers came, and owned large herds of horses and cattle. Chief Andrew passed down to his older son Peter the following history of their people, the Coeur d'Alene Indians. Upon Peter's death at a young age, this record was passed on to the younger son Joseph.

In Larry's book, *Northern Flight of Dreams*, he tells about spending his time as a boy at Chief Joseph Seltice's home and his friendship with the Chief and his grandchildren and a brief history of the Coeur d'Alene Indians.

184

Scott caught this salmon in Angoon, Alaska in 1981
while building a triplex for the school teachers there.
While attending WSU, he spent two summers in Alaska
as a builder.

Scott's wedding, January 18, 1987. Grandparents, Valmur, Jeanne Whitesitt, Stacy and Scott, Whitesitt.

Daniel and Kaitlyn catch their first fish at the Big Horn Sportsman Show, Spokane, Washington in front of their proud Grandpa Larry.

Daniel and puppy on Mineral Ridge Trail. While hiking with Grandpa
Larry at Lake Coeur d'Alene they met a couple with a puppy and they told
Daniel he could pick it up. Daniel looked up at me and said, "Grandpa
"How can I get a puppy?" I said, "We will work on it and found Hunter at a
kennel in the Spokane Valley.

Taking home Hunter, the yellow lab Daniel picked. Larry,
Stacy holding Hunter, Scott, Gavin, Daniel, and Kaitlyn.

Larry and grandson Daniel giving Larry's 'Huggin Tree' a bear hug. Daniel's 'huggin tree' is about 200' north along the same Liberty Creek Trail about a mile north of Liberty Lake. All of the grand children have 'huggin trees' close by.

The Whitesitt family, Stacy, Scott, Kaitlyn, Daniel, Gavin, and our wonderful dog, Hunter.

188

Larry Whitesitt on the left doing one of his talks and book signings that he has done about his adventures as a Bush Pilot, for almost 30 years.

Grant Brooks, pilot, Daniel sitting on Scott's lap, Stacy, Kaitlyn and Larry in the Beaver float plane N2106K flying over Lake Coeur d'Alene in the children's first plane ride and Stacy was pregnant with Gavin. About 16 years later Gavin would fly this Beaver off Lake Coeur d'Alene and Stacy and Larry would be sitting in the same middle seat as passengers.

Larry Whitesitt standing under the wing of the Beaver float plane N2106K that he and grandson Gavin flew off Lake Coeur d'Alene. Gavin flew the plane while his mother, Stacy and Larry sat in the middle seat. Gavin made a smooth happy landing, in this Beaver, The World's Best Bush Plane.

Daniel and Jordan Whitesitt's wedding with Daniel's grandparents. From left: Rita Hanson, Kathy Holt, Daniel, Jordan, and Larry Whitesitt

Gavin Whitesitt pumping water out of the floats as he prepares to take another flying lesson at Hayden Lake in this Piper J-3 Cub float plane. His instructor said he was a natural pilot. Gavin, his dad Scott and Grandpa Larry have all flown Piper J-3 Cubs and Beaver float planes, the Best Bush Plane in the world..

Daniel Whitesitt standing in front of his Great-Great-Grandfather Rydblom's cabin on Lake Coeur d'Alene where Larry spent his summers as a boy fishing with his grandpa Rydblom.

Daniel Whitesitt catching a perch in front of Grandpa Rydblom's cabin.
Harrison, Idaho is in the background

Daniel Whitesitt alongside Grandpa Larry's kayak going fishing. We
have spent many happy years together in our two kayaks fishing and
exploring since Daniel caught his first fish with me! Daniel is a true
fisherman like my grandfather William C. Rydblom who taught me
to fish. Daniel is a fly fisherman! This photo was taken at Upper Priest
Lake when we camped out for a few days in 2001 when Daniel was
about 9 years old. Gavin, my other grandson, and I kayaked to Upper
Priest Lake on a camping trip a few years later.

Grandson Daniel at age 12 and Larry. Daniel went with Larry and videotaped the interviews of World War II pilots that were in his book, *Higher Than Eagles: Spokane's World War II Pilots.*

Grandson Gavin Whitesitt's first flight in a glider next to his instructor at the Deer Park Airport.

Grandson Gavin Whitesitt and Larry at Felts Field Airport for Gavin's flight lesson in a Cessna 172.

Larry with grandson Gavin at the Kibby Dome, University of Idaho. Gavin received a scholarship to play football and graduated with a degree in Economics. He is now enrolled in a Master's Degree in Statistics (2019) at the university.

LARRY WHITESITT RECEIVES MASTER PILOT AWARD

LARRY LEE WHITESITT, EAA 1088285, of Fairfield, Washington, was honored with the FAA's Wright Brothers Master Pilot Award signifying 50 years of safe, violation-free flying—many as a bush pilot in Canada's Northwest Territory. Minard Thompson, FAASTeam program manager at the Spokane FSDO, presented the award at the Chapter 79 Christmas party held in December.

Larry, who at age 75 is current and still flies, has authored three books, including two recounting his bush-flying experiences. The first recounts what he calls his all-time favorite airplane, *Flight of the Red Beaver: A Yukon Bush Pilot Adventure*. The second book is *Northern Flight of Dreams: Flying Adventures* in British Columbia, Yukon, NW Territories and Alaska. He also wrote *Higher than Eagles: Spokane's World War II Pilots* in tribute to the heroes of WWII.

Larry receiving The Wright Brothers "Master Pilot: Award" for 50 years of safe flying from Minard Thompson.

Four pilots! Scott, Larry, Gavin, and Col Brian Newberry, the Commander of Fairchild Air Force Base, 92nd Air Refuelling Wing at our annual EAA Christmas Party on December 13, 2013 at the Spokane Valley Elks, when the FAA presented Larry with The Wright Brothers Master Pilot Award for 50+ years of Safe flying.

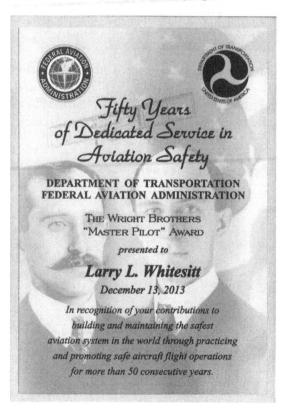

An article from the *Coeur d'Alene Press* introducing Daniel Whitesitt joining Lakeland Family Dental.

Daniel stands in front of the dental building where he began his practice in June 2019. Daniel's second patient was his brother Gavin Whitesitt!

Top: Jordan, Dr. Daniel, Gavin, Kaitlyn, Stacy, Scott and dog Maxwell.
The Whitesitt Family.

Index